MOVED

WITH

COMPASSION

KAY TOLMAN

Restoration Gateway Ministries

Moved with Compassion; A New Wineskin for Healing and Deliverance – Kay Tolman

Copyright © 2017

Scripture taken from the New King James Version. Copyright © 1982 Thomas Nelson, Inc., unless otherwise noted.

Printed in the United States of America

First edition published 2017
Published by:

Restoration Gateway Ministries

P.O Box 342
Beaverton, OR 97075
www.rgmconnect.com
Email: info@rgmconnect.com

ISBN-13: 978-0692946299

ISBN-10: 0692946292

Cover Design: April Beltran

Disclaimer: The information and suggestions offered in this book are intended to serve as guidelines only and not meant to preclude medical instruction.

Colossians 3:12 Amplified Bible

12 *So, as God's own chosen people, who are holy [set apart, sanctified for His purpose] and well-beloved [by God Himself], put on a heart of compassion, kindness, humility, gentleness, and patience [which has the power to endure whatever injustice or unpleasantness comes, with good temper].*

FOREWARD

BY DR. MARK VIKLER

Moved With Compassion by Kay Tolman is a long overdue book on the role of extending compassion as we minister healing. As she notes, Jesus, moved by compassion, healed (Matt. 14:14). It took me until age 64 to own a revelation concerning the importance of elevated emotion as the carrier wave of God's healing power. Spurgeon stated that the Gospel writers coined a new word to describe the intensity of the compassion Jesus had as He ministered healing. Previously, compassion was a noun. The Gospel writers turned it into a verb.

Wow, Spirit-born emotions which carry the power to heal! What a concept! The Kingdom of God is the emotions of peace and joy and the fruit of the Spirit includes emotions of love, joy, and peace (Rom 14:17; Gal. 5:22). These are Spirit-born emotions, or Kingdom emotions.

God sent Ezekiel, embittered in the rage of his spirit (Ezek. 3:14). Rage in one's spirit – Really? And all this time I thought emotions were soulish and had no place. Well, the Scriptures cited so far make it clear that emotions are spiritual and are to be honored. Talk about a life-transforming concept.

In my life's journey I have moved from scorning emotions, to accepting them, and now finally to honoring them. I believe I hinder the release of the Holy Spirit's healing power if I do not express the Spirit-born emotions of compassion, joy, peace, and gratitude.

So yes, it is high time we have books written about the centrality of the emotion of compassion in the ministry of healing, and this is one such book. As Kay demonstrates, we minister healing as we intensely love the person we are ministering to. If that compassion is not present, then we pray and ask God to plant His compassion within us. Now God's deliverance and healing can be released. Intense compassion is the switch that turns on God's healing power.

This book calls the Church to be the leader in compassionate healing prayer ministry. Let His gifts of faith and love flow together in your life. Let faith be energized by love (Gal. 5:6). Healing is the children's bread. Let us minister His compassionate healing touch to all we encounter.

As you read this book, make this your prayer: "Lord, birth within me Your compassion, so that Your healing power can flow fully and freely, accomplishing Your work!"

Dr. Mark Virkler

Co-author of *Unleashing Healing Power Through Spirit-Born Emotions*

DEDICATION

This book is dedicated to those who have been wounded in the care of Christian ministers. May the God of all comfort tend to your broken heart and bring healing and reconciliation in miraculous ways.

"Blessed be the God and Father of our LORD Jesus Christ, the Father of mercies and God of all comfort, who comforts us in all our tribulation, that we may be able to comfort those who are in any trouble, with the comfort with which we ourselves are comforted by God. For as the sufferings of Christ abound in us, so our consolation also abounds through Christ."

2 Corinthians 1:3-5

TABLE OF CONTENTS

ACKNOWLEDGEMENTS

With deepest gratitude, I would like to thank the LORD for the many people He brought along this journey, who encouraged and supported the efforts to complete this book.

First, I'd like to thank the many intercessors that believed in this concept and prayed it through to completion: including Deborah, Lou, Linda, Janice, Denise, Wendy, Jillian, Carolyn, Lauri, Jennifer, and Sharon.

Special thanks to Jennifer Rose and Lauri Smith for skillful editing and thoughtful contributions all along the way. Thanks also to Lauri Smith for her midwifery; co-laboring with me and helping me push through to delivery.

I would also like to thank my husband for his encouragement and perseverance with this project, while he did most of the chores. Finally, thank you to April for designing the cover and providing her professional support.

"I thank my God upon every remembrance of you…"

Philippians 1:3

INTRODUCTION

In my travels and ministry experience I have seen many wounded sheep that have been further wounded by ministers who attempted to help them. This ought not to be. Yet, I'm guilty of it myself and it grieves me deeply. More importantly, it grieves the heart of God. Moved with Compassion: a New Wine Skin for Healing and Deliverance, was birthed out of my desire to see compassion motivated ministry. I have set out to share what I have learned about emotional care, healing, and deliverance in the hope that others may benefit and safely be restored.

Although I am not a biblical scholar, I do believe the Word of God is authoritative and the basis for truth. Hence, you will find a lot of scripture within these pages. I believe the scripture is more than mere words on a page; it has a transforming power that brings renewal to the mind, body, soul, and spirit.

In my discourse on the new wineskin it is not my heart to diminish the work of those who have blazed the path before me. Instead, I hope to build upon established truth so the body of Christ can move forward into more of what our Heavenly Father has for us today. Over the years, revelation has unfolded and many wonderful ministries have published brave and pioneering works about deliverance and healing ministry. We have come a long way in our quest to understand the freedom Christ purchased for us on the cross of Calvary. The Holy Spirit wants to release greater spiritual insight to the Body of Christ in this hour, it is my hope you may find some of it in this work. We can't become complacent with the former things because the revelation given yesterday was for a different season.

We live in perilous times when deception and deep darkness cover the earth. Unlike any other period in history our discernment must be razor sharp or even the elect may be deceived. I believe the Church will face evil in ways we have never seen before. The devil knows his time is short. To triumph we need a fresh equipping, new tools, and strategies directly from the throne room for such a time as this. We need a baptism of love and compassion so we can walk as Jesus walked and move as Jesus moved. We need a divine transfiguration, leaving our flesh behind to become Jesus with skin on to a lost and hurting world. May we have ears to hear what the Spirit is saying to the Churches.

"Do not remember the former things, nor consider the things of old. Behold, I will do a new thing, now it shall spring forth; shall you not know it?"

Isaiah 43:18-19

CHAPTER 1

MOVED WITH COMPASSION

Wherever you look, lost and hurting souls are crying out in distress for a touch from God. They are Christians and non-Christians alike. You can see it in their eyes, you can hear it in their words. It is reminiscent of Romans 8:22, *"For we know the whole creation groans and labors with birth pangs together until now."* Despite human advancements, or possibly as the result of those advancements, people need love and compassion more now than ever before.

Regardless of occupation or status in life, Christians are all called to minister love and compassion. I believe ministry starts at home and love should extend to every area of our influence whether at the workplace, the university, the church, or the grocery store. Most especially love is the cornerstone for ministering healing and deliverance. In John 13:35, Jesus said, *"By this all will know that you are My disciples, if you have love for one another."*

DEFINING COMPASSION

It was said of Jesus in Matthew 9:36, *"... when He saw the multitudes, He was moved with compassion for them, because they were weary and scattered, like sheep having no shepherd."*

The term compassion literally means "to suffer together." This could be what Paul meant when he said, "Rejoice with those who rejoice, and weep with those who weep" (Romans 12:15).

Strong's Exhaustive Concordance of the Bible notes several definitions of the word "compassion." It means to commiserate or to spare (#2550); tender mercy (#3627); to love, show mercy and have pity (#7355); and full of compassion (#7349).

Merriam Webster defines compassion as "sympathetic consciousness of others, distress together with a desire to alleviate it."[1]

The researchers at UC Berkley have this to say about compassion. "While cynics may dismiss compassion as touchy-feely or irrational, research has shown that when we feel compassion, our heart rate slows down, we secrete the "bonding hormone" oxytocin, and regions of the brain linked to empathy, caregiving, and feelings of pleasure light up, which often results in our wanting to approach and care for other people." [2]

Whether it is brain chemistry or the prompting of the Holy Spirit, compassion is like a catalyst that motivates us to love and extend God's tender mercy.

The antonym for compassion is cruelty or indifference. Most people are not intentionally cruel, but how often are we indifferent to the sufferings of others? Haven't we all dismissed people's feelings or avoided those obviously in pain?

JESUS, THE HEALER

The scripture says in Matthew 4:23, *"And Jesus went about all Galilee, teaching in their synagogues, preaching the gospel of the kingdom, and healing all kinds of sickness and all kinds of disease among the people."* Verse 24, *"…and they brought to Him all sick people who*

---

1   https://www.merriam-webster.com/dictionary/compassion 3.1.17

2   http://greatergood.berkeley.edu/topic/compassion/definition 12.15.16

were afflicted with various diseases and torments, and those who were demon-possessed, epileptics and paralytics; and He healed them." Isn't it interesting how the Holy Spirit linked physical healing together with deliverance from evil spirits and termed it all "healing" in this passage?

John 14:12 states, *"Most assuredly, I say to you, he who believes in Me, the works that I do he will do also; and greater works than these he will do, because I go to My Father."* Isn't that exciting? God is equipping us to do even greater works than these!

If we are to minister like Jesus and to become people that are Jesus with "skin on" for others, we must fix our eyes upon Him. 2 Corinthians 3:17-18 says, *"Now the LORD is the Spirit; and where the Spirit of the LORD is, there is liberty. But we all, with unveiled face, beholding as in a mirror the glory of the LORD, are being transformed into the same image from glory to glory, just as by the Spirit of the LORD."* As we fix our eyes on Jesus, the author and finisher of our faith (Hebrews 12:2), we are transformed into His image (2 Cor. 3:18). Wow, that's powerful!

I like to imagine the look in Jesus' eyes while He ministered to hurting people. What was He thinking? What was He feeling? Look closely, His eyes are indescribably amazing!

Picture yourself standing next to Jesus when he approached the man of the Gadarenes in Mark chapter 5. The man is filthy and unclothed. Oppression and heaviness cover him like a dark cloud of soot as he emerges from the tombs crying out in anguish. He's in so much pain he has cut himself for relief. Chained and bloody, he runs toward Jesus.

Jesus can feel his pain and He is moved with compassion toward him. The man falls at Jesus' feet to worship Him. But in the presence of His holiness the demons manifest and speak from his mouth.

Can you imagine how ashamed the man from Gadarenes felt in that moment?

Jesus seems unruffled. He simply commands the unclean spirit out, then He addresses the legion of spirits, and casts them out as well. Jesus says gently, *"Go home to your friends and tell them what great things the LORD has done for you and how He has had compassion on you"* (Mark 5:19).

Although the book of Mark is the shortest gospel account (Mark likes to get to the point quickly), his rendering of this story is the only one that mentions the words, "He has had compassion on you." That seems noteworthy.

My favorite part of the story is when the witnesses to this event came to Jesus in Mark 5:15. They described how they saw the one who had been demon-possessed and had the legion, sitting and clothed and in his right mind. It's a deliverance promise that saw me through many years of my own torment and tears.

Jesus, our model for healing and deliverance, was moved with compassion as He healed. Although He had human needs He didn't operate out of His fleshly nature. And he didn't need to wield a big fancy sword or boast about His authority. Although, He was given all authority in Ephesians 1:20-23. He carried the sword of Hebrews 4:12, which could discern the thoughts and intents of the heart. He embodied these things and He moved in love. He was motivated by love.

EMOTIONAL CARE

Most Christians believe they minister out of love, but they lack the knowledge and tools to properly address emotional needs. And there is a difference between ministering from human love and flowing from the Father's love. Over the years I've heard many people report having been wounded by Christian ministers wielding a big deliverance sword and boasting in their authority. Although they believe these ministers were sincerely doing the best they could to help them, the wounding was deep.

The following chapters were written to equip ministers to provide better emotional care and more effective deliverance strategies. You will glean new tools and insight to prevent causing emotional harm and instead help people resolve recurrent issues. Most importantly, you will learn how to release the love of God into the deepest places of the heart to facilitate lasting freedom, deliverance, and restoration.

The Spirit is calling the Church to an even more effective level of compassionate ministry. The new wineskin for ministry is free of judgment, criticism, legalism, and shame. It listens; it really hears the heart. The new wineskin puts emotional care before deliverance procedures and speaks the truth in love. It accepts people where they are right now with grace and mercy, while trusting the Holy Spirit to bring them to full repentance. Ministers of the new wineskin will teach people how to hear God's voice for themselves (John 10:27) and how to get their emotional needs met directly from Him, rather than allowing co-dependence to operate in the ministry relationship.

THE WINESKIN

The old wineskin for healing and deliverance will not hold the new wine for today (Matthew 9:17). When God pours out His Spirit on all flesh (Acts 2:17) it won't look like Church as usual!

We are on the threshold of a global harvest. People of all ethnicities, belief systems, and cultures will be responding to the gospel. Out of deep darkness, witchcraft, and perversity, they will come to Christ. When they do, will we know how to really love them?

It's not enough to know of Jesus. No, to live worthy of a ministry calling requires intimate fellowship with our Beloved. As we draw nearer to Him, as we fix our eyes upon Jesus, we are transformed into His image, from glory to glory (2 Corinthians 3:18). If we want to minister as Jesus did, we must develop more than an understanding of His methods; we also need to develop a sense of His feelings, because the most effective ministry flows from the heart of God. What is required of us to love and move with compassion like Jesus did? We require an immersion in His love. Then, with an open heart, we must allow ourselves to feel and be emotionally present in the moment so we can serve as conduits of His love.

Wouldn't you like to walk in the same love from our Heavenly Father as the Father has for Jesus? You can. I call it the baptism of love and from it flows the miraculous.

"You've kept track of all my wandering and my weeping. You've stored my many tears in your bottle – not one will be lost. You care about me every time I've cried. For it is all recorded in Your book of remembrance."

Psalm 56:8 - Passion Translation

CHAPTER 2

THE BAPTISM OF LOVE

Like many people in ministry, I was released into my calling after a long and arduous personal journey of restoration. As a survivor of satanic ritual abuse, I could relate to the man of the Gadarenes. I spent nineteen years in therapy and five years with various deliverance ministers seeking freedom and the promise of a sound mind. When I was nearly hopeless and at the end of my rope, God brought me to George.

During one of our ministry sessions, George said to me, "Katie you can't love others because you don't love yourself." (Holy Spirit calls me Katie.)

His words hit me hard. "Of course, I love others!" I replied defensively.

"Well," he said reaching for his Bible. "It says right here, in Luke 10:27, *'You shall love the LORD your God with all your heart, with all your soul, with all your strength, and with all your mind, and your neighbor as yourself.'* Until you learn to love yourself you can't really love other people."

I started crying and replied honestly, "I don't know how to love myself."

George has an amazing prophetic gift to see into the heart of those he ministers to. He described seeing my heart as a vault with chains around it. "Katie," he said, "You can't let the love in."

He was right. I had been so wounded in relationships, I believed love would hurt me again. As a matter of self-preservation, I had sealed my heart shut like Fort Knox. No love could come in and no love could flow out. I had deceived myself into believing kindness was a substitute for real love.

Ezekiel 36:26 provides hope. The Spirit of the LORD says, *"I will give you a new heart and put a new spirit within you; I will take the heart of stone out of your flesh and give you a heart of flesh."*

Together we prayed. George said, "Repeat after me, Heavenly Father, will you put a love in my heart for me like You love me? Father, I open my heart to receive from You, in Jesus Name."

I pictured my heart opening and the chains coming loose. Then I fixed my eyes on Jesus (Hebrews 12:2). In my mind's eye, Jesus had my hand and He led me up the steps to a great throne where my Heavenly Father sat beaming. Seemingly, I was a child of 7 or 8 years old again, sitting on my Father's lap. In that moment, I felt the love of my Heavenly Father permeate my entire being. I can't explain the experience except to say from that moment on I knew, that I knew, that I was loved. The love so radically changed me, I could love myself and honestly love others too, for the very first time. From that moment on I was ruined for human substitutes.

Not everyone has a George nearby to pray with them. But in the same way we receive the baptism of the Holy Spirit, simply by asking in faith, we can receive the baptism of love. The term "baptism of love" isn't found in scripture. But Jesus did say, *"By this all will know that you are My disciples, if you have love for one another"* (John 13:35). Similar to other biblical forms of baptism an immersion in the Father's love deeply changes a person. This is a good gift that the Father delights to give His children. Without the love from God we can't fulfill the greatest commandment and we won't be moved with the compassion of Christ to serve a lost and hurting world.

Several months after receiving the baptism of love, George invited me to join his ministry. He said, "I always look for the baptism of love to determine if someone is a fit for the ministry. It is the most important qualifying factor." I do believe George was right.

AUTHENTIC LOVE

In our humanity, our brokenness, rejection, and abandonment, our affections are self-serving and inadequate. But love from the Spirit of God will cause us to lay our lives down for another. Authentic love will not enable, it doesn't ignore problems, but will confront sin. Love doesn't demand its own way, but respects choices. True love is unconditional, accepting, and rare.

The late prophet Bob Jones spoke at a conference in Albany, Oregon, in 2006. He shared a testimony of his 1976 near-death experience in the heavenly throne room. He said, "I watched the LORD speak to people that were coming there. And He asked them only one question: 'Did you learn to love?'" Bob went on to tell his audience, "He's not going to ask you what you did. If you learn to love you are going to do that which is right."[3]

Love, the currency of heaven, changes things here on earth. It is by far the greatest gift of all. The Apostle Paul was acquainted with these truths when he wrote 1 Corinthians chapter 13.

Though I speak with the tongues of men and of angels, but have not love, I have become sounding brass or a clanging symbol.

And though I have the gift of prophecy and understand all mysteries and all knowledge, and

---

3   http://www.elijahlist.com/words/display_word.html?ID=13128

though I have all faith, so that I could remove mountains, but have not love, I am nothing.

And though I bestow all my goods to feed the poor, and though I give my body to be burned, but have not love, it profits me nothing.

Love suffers long and is kind; love does not envy; love does not parade itself, is not puffed up; does not behave rudely, does not seek its own, is not provoked, thinks no evil; does not rejoice in iniquity, but rejoices in the truth;

Bears all things, believes all things, hopes all things, endures all things.

Love never fails.

CHAPTER 3

STOICISM IN THE CHURCH

In the New York Times best seller, "Living Beyond your Feelings," Joyce Meyer writes in the first paragraph, "It has been said that emotions are the Christian's number one enemy because they can easily prevent us from following the will of God." Later in the first chapter, she writes, "Our feelings are unreliable and cannot be trusted to convey the truth."

In Western culture, we tend to look very negatively at emotions. We've been taught not to trust our feelings, that they are the enemy of the rational mind, pitting us against the will of God as a thorn in our flesh. Our Greek mindset bows to reason and denies the simplest of feelings as though this were an act of virtue unto God.

Most people have been taught to suppress, deny, and avoid negative feelings their entire lives. When a child feels angry parents often punish their children. It sometimes starts in the home when a parent says, "Stop your crying or I'll give you something to cry about!" And as a child gets older their peers will mock or humiliate them for expressing feelings in school. And right from the pulpit priests and pastors have been teaching their congregations to deny their feelings and allow reason to rule them for hundreds of years.

Where did this abhorrence of emotions come from? Where did we get the idea that we must not express our feelings, especially in church? I believe this idea is rooted in the Hellenistic school of philosophy called "Stoicism", founded by Zeno in Athens, 300 years before Christ.[4] Stoics taught that emotions are destructive and could result in errors of judgment.

Today, the word stoic "refers to someone who is unemotional or indifferent to pain, pleasure, grief or joy..."[5] This belief is rooted in paganism, not the Holy Bible.

"Stoicism teaches the development of self-control and fortitude as a means of overcoming destructive emotions; the philosophy holds that becoming a clear and unbiased thinker allows one to understand the universal reason,"[4] says Wikipedia. Here we find the full embodiment of the Greek mindset that has pervaded our homes, our educational systems, and our pulpits for centuries. Stoicism aligns with Classical Theology and the belief that God is distant, detached, unapproachable, and unemotional, and thereby indifferent to our feelings. But that is not what the Word of God reveals. In Harold Eberle's extraordinary book "Systematic Theology for the New Apostolic Reformation; An Exposition in Father-Son Theology," the author unpacks these concepts with precision. I encourage the reader to include this work in their further study on this theological subject.

EMOTIONAL INTIMACY WITH GOD

The God of Abraham, Isaac and Jacob cares deeply for our feelings and longs to bring healing and restoration to every area of our lives. In Jeremiah 31, God turns mourning into joy and tells his people in verse 3, *"I have loved you with an everlasting love; therefore, with lovingkindness I have drawn you and continued My faithfulness to you"* (AMP).

---

4   https://en.wikipedia.org/wiki/Stoicism

5   http://www.philosophybasics.com/branch_stoicism.html

In 1 Peter 5:7, God instructs us to cast all our cares, all our anxieties, worries and concerns, once and for all on Him, because He cares with deepest affection and watches over each one of us very carefully (AMP version). That doesn't sound like a distant and indifferent God. Rather One that is deeply engaged in our lives and intimately concerned for what concerns us. He emphatically declares, *"I am my beloved's and my beloved is mine"* (Song of Solomon 6:3).

We are so deeply loved. He implores us to love others out of the deepest intimacy we have with Him. To touch the world for Christ requires a revelation of His love. How can we minister without it?

George used to say, "Intimacy means, into me see." Emotional intimacy requires the opening of the heart. Like the ancient doors to the temple in Jerusalem, we can enter the temple, past the outer court, into the inner court, where the lamp of God reveals the hidden chambers of the soul. This is where we lay our lives down at the brazen altar and lift our prayers at the altar of incense. As we press in deeper, beyond the veil, it is spiritual encounter in the Holy of Holies where words fail us. Just imagine stepping into the presence of God, being one with Him, in the Holy of Holies. Selah (pause).

"… the one who joins himself to the LORD is one spirit with Him" (1 Cor. 6:17). Can you just imagine your spirit fused together with His Spirit! That fusion is like a nuclear encounter! If we operate out of this intimate fusion with God's spirit and His love, miraculous possibilities are endless.

ARE FEELINGS A SIN?

Is it a sin to experience emotions? No, you can't prove that from the Bible, but you might get that idea from the current mindset in the Church. Some equate emotions with the "works of the flesh" (Gal. 5:19-21) and vehemently argue against them. But I would counter this concept with the fact that both our spirit and the Holy Spirit have emotions. Here are some examples: Isaiah 63:10, "But they rebelled and grieved His Holy Spirit." Romans 14:17, "For the kingdom of God is not eating and drinking, but righteousness and peace and joy in the Holy Spirit."

The most familiar scripture describing the emotions evident in the Holy Spirit is Galatians 5:22, *"But the fruit of the Spirit is love, joy, peace, longsuffering, kindness, goodness, faithfulness, gentleness, self-control. Against such there is no law."*

In most deliverance circles, if you express anger they will think you need deliverance. "Cast out that spirit of anger!" they say. But Paul said, *"Be angry and do not sin; do not let the sun go down on your wrath"* (Ephesians 4:26). What is Paul saying? Experience your anger but don't hurt anyone with it. Don't repress it or hang on to it. Process it today.

What about fear? Human beings were wired by their Creator to experience fear. When a person perceives danger, it is normal to feel fear. Be careful admitting this feeling around ministers, you are likely to get a sermon on the difference between faith and fear that completely discounts your feelings. Somehow the Church needs to learn to differentiate between normal human emotions and demonic strongholds. I think the best way to do that is to lovingly care for and acknowledge feelings as the gift of God that they are, before engaging in spiritual warfare and trying to cast them out! This is the juncture where psychologists and the medical community provide safer emotional recovery than the Church. I believe this grieves the heart of God, as such, He desires to create in us a new wineskin for healing and deliverance that ministers to emotions skillfully.

DENYING OUR FEELINGS

If God values our feelings and desires a love relationship with us, what is the price we pay for stoic self-denial? When we deny our feelings, we deny an essential aspect of who we are. We lose touch with our authentic self. Stoicism implies that feelings are not acceptable or true. Therefore, we deny them, stuff them away and reject our own voice as unacceptable. This can breed self-rejection, self-condemnation, and in some cases, severe depression. Like trying to hold a beach ball under water, the feelings will naturally try to surface. What do we do? We may stuff them down with food, have another glass of wine, run up our credit card, or stay late at work. Unresolved emotions are a breeding ground for addiction. Is it any wonder addiction rates in the Church are so high?

When we suppress or repress our feelings we lose the good ones too. Emotions are not like a salad bar where we can pick and choose what appeals to us. When the negative emotions are battered down, joy also escapes us, and depression lingers on long after times of sorrow. For survivors of severe trauma and abuse, stoicism hinders recovery and is every bit as abusive as the perpetrator that demands silence. The doors to the heart are locked and chains secure them decisively.

I'm not suggesting we act on every impulse or indulge every whim of our emotions. I am saying that we must pay attention to our emotions. Feelings can be like a light on the dashboard of your car. You can ignore the check engine light for awhile, but it won't be long before you have a problem. When people don't acknowledge their deeply held feelings they can experience physical ailments. There are emotional roots to most physical maladies because the *body speaks for the emotions when they aren't given a voice.*

When I was a child I suffered from severe asthma. Fear, stress and anxiety were certainly the emotional root as described in Henry Wright's "A More Excellent Way". But on an even deeper level, due to the severe trauma in my childhood, I couldn't take in life, I couldn't breathe it in. Life was too painful and terrifying. If someone had said to me, "just cast out that spirit of fear! Repent!" Can you imagine how I would have felt?

Today the "ruach" (Strong's #7307) or breath of the Holy Spirit fills my lungs and I can breathe. The trauma and deeply buried emotions of long ago have been processed and every breath in my body is for the glory of God. I can run the race set before me and you can too.

GREEK VS HEBREW MINDSETS

A good contrast between the Greek stoic mindset and the Hebrew (Biblical) mindset is seen in how each culture manages grief. In Western culture, we tend to postpone our grief or dismiss it altogether. When someone we love dies, we have three days off and back to work we go. Our well-meaning Christian friends and family say pithy things like, "He's in a better place. Move on with your life. Forget the past."

But in Hebrew culture, grief is taken very seriously. There are four set periods of mourning. The first is the most intense period between death and burial known as *aninut*. The seven-day period after burial is more commonly known as *shiva*. During this time mourners stay home and receive the love and comfort of loved ones. Mirrors are covered so mourners don't have to look good. Prayers are recited, memorial candles are lit, and a ribbon or torn clothing may be worn to signify the loss. The third period, *sheloshim*, incorporates the first seven days and continues for a month. And finally, there is a recognized year of mourning. Within these set times people are encouraged to grieve and are given support to do so.[6]

In our modern Greek culture, the thought of expressing feelings for 30 days seems unreasonable even abhorrent. But God knows how He created us. He knows we need to grieve. Did you know in the ancient Middle East there was a practice of hiring mourners? In Jeremiah 9:17-18, the Word says, *"Thus says the LORD of hosts, 'Consider and call for the mourning women, that they may come; and send for the wailing women, that they may come! And let them make haste, and take up a wailing for us, that our eyes may shed tears, and our eyelids flow with water.'"*

EMOTIONAL BURDENS

When I was nineteen, my father died of lung cancer. I walked around in a daze for a couple of days, then returned to my job. I didn't know how to process my grief, so I stuffed it away and busied myself with wedding plans. Two years later when the marriage ended, the grief over the loss of my father came over me suddenly, like a surprise tsunami. The feelings hadn't gone away because I didn't allow myself to process them. *Time doesn't heal repressed feelings.*

We weren't designed to carry the baggage of repressed emotions. God didn't design us as beasts of burden like mules or camels. He calls us sheep. Did you know that sheep can fall over if their wool gets too thick? Sheep were never designed to carry burdens, and neither are we. *"Cast your burden upon the LORD, and He will sustain you"* (Psalm 55:22).

---

6   http://www.shiva.com/learning-center/understanding/periods-of-mourning/

I remember the first time I felt authentic joy; I was 43 years old and it was so unfamiliar to me, I wasn't sure what it was. After unpacking decades of repressed emotions, and living abstinent with food addiction, joy suddenly began to bubble up within me. It reminded me of this Scripture, *"So the ransomed of the LORD shall return, and come to Zion with singing, with everlasting joy on their heads, they shall obtain joy and gladness; sorrow and sighing shall flee away"* (Isaiah 51:11).

By learning to care for our own feelings, we can learn to tenderly care for the emotions of those we serve. There is a place and a time for grappling with deep emotions and there is a difference between acknowledging our feelings, and indiscriminately blasting people with them like a fire hose. I dare say, most people need to learn how to process feelings appropriately. When our emotions are cared for, they are much easier to manage and we can fully engage in life, free to be who we are, authentically. If we properly address our feelings, we can work through them with the Holy Spirit and they will not consume us, we can heal. In chapter 9, we will discuss how to safely process emotions.

THE HEART OF GOD

We have been created in the image of God (Gen. 1:27). We are each like a magnificent jewel in His crown, a unique reflection of His glory and creativity (Zech. 9:16). When He shines within us, His light is reflected in each precise etching, each colorful prism. As such, our lives are very precious to Him.

He smiles over us like a delighted parent over a newborn baby. He counts each finger and toe, and every hair on our head is numbered (Matt. 10:30). Just like any good parent, He has strong feelings about our lives; how we should grow, be cared for and protected. And He is jealous for our affections because He knows how easily we can be led astray (Exodus 34:14).

The God of all creation is described in the Bible as having a full range of emotions, just like we do. He laughs (Psalm 37:13); He cries (John 11:35); and He experiences sorrow and grief as it is written in Genesis 6:6, *"And the LORD was sorry that He had made man on the earth, and He was grieved in His heart."* In Ephesians 4:30 we discover the Holy Spirit grieves too.

The wrath of God described in the Old Testament is well known. One example is Numbers 25:11, *"Phinehas the son of Eleazar, the son of Aaron the priest, has turned back My wrath from the children of Israel, because he was zealous with My zeal among them, so that I did not consume the children of Israel in My zeal."*

In John 2:15, Jesus made a whip of cords, and drove the money changers out of the temple with their sheep and the oxen, and overturned the tables! His disciples remembered that it was written, *"Zeal for your house has eaten me up"* (John 2:17). This isn't the picture of the stoic Jesus that many would like to presume exists; carefully controlled and emotionless. No, He was passionate and forceful as He tore the place up!

In Zephaniah 3:17, God also expresses joyous feelings. *"He will rejoice over you with gladness, He will quiet you with His love, He will rejoice over you with singing."*

We can see that God gets angry, He grieves, He's zealous, He feels glad and rejoices. These are important characteristics of God, through which we can also value our own emotions.

EMOTIONAL HEALING WITH JESUS

Some years back, a person I trusted in my ministry, someone whom

I had given five years of my life as a minister, one I considered a friend, seriously betrayed me. She had been in my home for holiday meals. She helped with the church and was on the leadership team. She even had keys to my office which she used to hold a satanic ritual. Upon the realization, my heart broke. I took the necessary steps to change locks, clean the defilement from my office, and remove her from the leadership team. We discontinued communication and I went on with my very busy life hardened and angry inside. At the time, I was also taking a class for my Master's degree. My assignment was to spend some time with Jesus and allow Him to minister to me.

On a quiet Sunday afternoon, I closed my eyes and pictured Jesus in my mind's eye. We were in an attic in the scene and He was sitting in a big rocking chair weeping. As you might imagine the attic was littered with boxes and old things. He motioned to me to pick up a big white box and give it to Him. I reached for the box and said, "What's in here Jesus?" Tears were streaming down His face and He replied, "It's time my child to open that box and have your feelings. Sit on my lap and let me hold you in the rocking chair."

I told Jesus I was angry about the betrayal but underneath the anger was deep pain. I let Him hold me, rocking back and forth until the feelings were spent.

In Acts 13:22 The LORD said, *"I have found David the son of Jesse, a man after My own heart, who will do all My will."* David is the only Biblical character that received this honor. If you read the Psalms you can't help but conclude David experienced a full range of emotions too. David poured his heart out to God and then strengthened himself in faith and trust in Him.

Just like our Father in Heaven, and just like Jesus, we were designed with emotions. Mercurial and unpredictable, emotions can be very challenging and messy for even the most seasoned saint. But our feelings are dear to the heart of God. As a matter of fact, the area of our brain that experiences emotion is also the area of the brain through which we experience Him. The new wineskin for healing and deliverance requires us to intimately know Him so we can minister in and through His presence. In the process, we must learn how to care for emotions.

Throughout history, stoicism has only served to separate us from our Creator and to deny us our true feelings. It is my hope that the Body of Christ will learn to embrace emotions and lovingly serve the world around us out of the love with which Christ first loved us.

"We love Him because He first loved us."

1 John 4:19

CHAPTER 4

LEFT AND RIGHT BRAIN PROCESSING

God wired our brain with two hemispheres, right and left. Each hemisphere operates differently but in concert with each other. It is helpful to understand the differences in each hemisphere when ministering to emotions and deep inner wounding.

The left hemisphere of the brain operates the right hand. Most people are right handed and left brained. The left brain is primarily used in logical processes such as mathematics, language and the ordering of facts. The left brain uses analysis, calculation, and reasoning. This is the seat of the intellectual mind. This area of the brain really begins to develop as a child nears four, five and six years old when they learn to read. Most of our Western educational systems have developed from a Greek mindset, where the focus is on left brain analytical endeavors such as science, mathematics, and language.

In contrast, the right brain is creative, emotional, and intuitive, which is more conducive to a Hebrew mindset, using symbols and pictures. Right brain dominant processors are likely to be left handed or sometimes ambidextrous, especially if they have been forced to use their right hand to push a pencil in school. The right brain is the seat of the emotions, imagination, and the place where we experience God. The revelatory gifts of the Holy Spirit, such as prophecy, visions, and even tongues, all move through the functions of the right brain. The easier people can move between right and left-brain hemispheres, the more effectively they can utilize all their God given ability.

If I want my audience to feel and experience what I am saying, I use word pictures, as in previous chapters. If I simply want to convey facts and figures, I will appeal to the analytical left brain and present a detailed case in logical order. To be most effective, I use both.

Have you ever heard the expression, "The longest eighteen inches is from your head to your heart?" People often struggle to get the truth of scripture from head knowledge to experiential heart affirming truth. This is the difference between left and right brain processing. If a person has shut off their feelings, they will have a more difficult time connecting with God. Music and praise open the heart and the emotions to enable us to connect with God and receive His truth. This is the reason we sing and worship in church before the preaching begins. If the sermon is simply factual, void of feeling or tone, we tune out and may completely miss the point.

Transitioning from left brain mode into right brain mode can bring the Bible to life by moving the words into pictures, the message will speak to the emotions of the heart. Have you ever sat down to read the Bible and after fifteen minutes you have no idea what you just read? If that is the case you were reading using your left brain. If you really want to experience the scripture and have it come to life, you need to picture what you are reading. Take the story of the woman at the well, in Luke chapter 4, as an example. If this chapter was simply read as a left-brain exercise, you would know about the woman at the well from the text, but wouldn't see her. Instead, if you could picture the stones around the well and see a woman with long brown hair sitting next to Jesus, it would come to life!

Right brain processing could be described like watercolors, abstract and flowing. Whereas left brain processing is more like typed text, it is linear with defined edges, like a spreadsheet. Left brain dominant processors tend to work from the bottom up, details first. Good examples of left-brain professions are accounting, engineering, and scientific research.

Learning music is an important way to develop both left and right hemispheres. Musical instruments require the use of both right and left hands and combine both musical notation (left), with melodious sound (right). Music, art, drama, and similar creative activities all utilize the right brain. Interestingly, and unfortunately, when school administrators cut budgets these subjects are usually the first go. Studies show children that learn music and the arts in school are much more likely to succeed academically.

Right brain thinkers tend to see the world in terms of the big picture, top down. Many of our US presidents have been left handed and right brain dominant. The most successful leaders, sales professionals, hair stylists, photographers, actors, and artists are usually right brainers.

The most beloved teachers can speak to both hemispheres of the brain, bringing both facts, and creativity into each lesson plan. The more colorful and creative the lesson, the greater the degree with which students will learn and engage.

Marketers that want to sell new cars will combine both facts about the cars' performance with pictures that evoke emotion. The more emotion a marketing genius can evoke in their advertising, the more likely the ad will stick with you and prompt you to buy the car. During Super Bowl advertising costs are at a premium and you may notice every commercial is colorful and plays on your emotions. Have you seen the ad with the dog driving the safe new car in the middle of the night, so the puppy will fall asleep in the back seat? Been there, done that, I want that car!

Our dream state is also a right brain process. When we are asleep, the analytical intellectual mind rests, while the heart processes pictures and feelings. Have you noticed when you have a lot of things on your mind it is difficult to sleep? To get into the sweet peaceful sleep we need to quiet the busy analytical mind.

Why is this important in ministry? Because the things we believe, the emotions we feel, the trauma that seeks resolution, is all in the right brain. You can read about God and not know Him. Or you can experience Him with your spirit and soul and be forever changed. It's a little like the difference between reading the driver's manual and literally driving the car. The most effective ministry activates the capacity of the right hemisphere of the brain where Jesus Himself does the healing of the broken heart.

For further study on this topic I highly recommend "4 Keys to Hearing God's Voice" by Mark and Patti Virkler.

To discover more about brain preferences, do an internet search on "brain preference indicator test." There are a variety of tests available online to help you and your clients discover which hemisphere of the brain is most dominant. Ideally, you want to work toward a good healthy balance between right and left-brain function.

CHAPTER 5

WOUNDED IN CHRISTIAN CARE

One of the things I often hear as a minister is the pain of people that have been hurt in the care of Christian pastors, ministers, and friends. Sometimes it is the result of ignorance, other times it is a matter of willful neglect or abuse. Most often, however, ministers don't realize they are hurting those entrusted to their care. But ministry in the Name of Jesus is a sacred trust between the minister and the LORD Himself, and the ministry recipient. It's like a three-fold cord. Together in harmony, the cord is strong. However, any violation of that trust can cause a cascade of effects that can lead to lasting trauma and bondage in a person's life.

The biggest offenders of the sacred trust include the following characteristics: pride, shame, judgment, criticism, legalism and a religious or pharisaical spirit. A pharisaical spirit is defined as "Practicing or advocating strict observance of external forms and ceremonies of religion or conduct without regard to the Spirit; self-righteous; hypocritical."[7] Each of these attitudes routinely precludes sensitivity to emotional considerations as well.

LISTEN AND LOVE

We need to learn how to meet with people, right where they are and hear their heavy hearts. When we do, we become a container, a vessel for them. Listening can be the very best medicine. To have ears that really hear you must be emotionally present with no agenda. Limit distractions and make eye contact. Don't offer advice or give instructions, just be in the moment. The less said,

---

7   http://www.dictionary.com/browse/pharisaical

the better. Allow yourself to feel. You become a container as the hurting pour out their heart.

While visiting a friend recently, I met a young woman visiting from out of town. She was sweet and warm, a precious saint. She had been deeply wounded by ministers and people in the church, but I offered to pray for her anyway. She reluctantly accepted. Sensing her distrust, I just imagined the love of Christ for her and let it rise-up through me like living water. As she gingerly opened her heart, I listened intently. She watched my face for any signs of judgment or criticism. When none came, she allowed herself to share more. When we prayed, Jesus moved mightily to bring healing and freedom to her broken heart.

Later she shared that it was simply the love and compassion she felt from me that enabled her to receive ministry. This left me wondering how many people could be touched by the love of God and receive the healing they long for, if only ministers were emotionally safer.

A similar example occurred recently when a young man came to see me on behalf of his little boy. As I spoke to this young father I wondered about the pain in his life. I asked him, "Do you have any support with all of the challenges you are facing?" He shook his head "no."

He then proceeded to tell me how he had been hurt in church and by ministers. He explained that his heart couldn't take one more wounding, rather than risk it, he preferred to isolate. We continued our discussion and I listened intently without judgment. He was suffering from PTSD and had a background involving street drugs, gang activity, and prison. Although he had turned his life around, he was using both medications and marijuana for pain and anxiety relief, both physical and emotional. Now at this juncture, I could have scolded him for those choices and given him a lecture on the "open door" those things were creating in his life. Instead, I deferred to the Holy Spirit, with full confidence, knowing He would lead this young man to repentance and freedom when the time was right.

I said, "God can heal these areas in your life. God can heal PTSD and He can take the emotional pain. When that happens, you won't need those other substances. When the Holy Spirit puts His finger on those things in your life, you will be able to put them down."

Relieved at my response, he admitted these substances were creating a problem in his relationship with God and he was thinking about quitting. The best part was that he agreed to come back and see me. That was the "open door" God wanted to create.

These two examples demonstrate how unresolved hurt from those in the ministry can leave people separated from believers and stuck in their shackles and pain. If ministers will only hear the wounded heart and respond with love and mercy, we may become the bridge builders and peace makers God intended us to be.

"And those from among you will rebuild the ancient ruins, you will raise up the age-old foundations; and you will be called the repairer of the breach, the restorer of the streets in which to dwell" (Isaiah 58:12).

SIN CONSCIOUS VS GOD CONSCIOUS

Working in deliverance ministry, it is easy to get legalistic. We can see what causes bondage in a person's life and how the enemy can get a foothold. Things can seem black and white, right and wrong. Sin is sin. We can even become very sin conscious trying to eradicate every trace of the enemy out from behind every rock. But that is when we run into the danger of becoming legalistic.

Remember the Pharisees? Jesus called them blind guides, *"who strain out a gnat and swallow a camel"* (Matt 23:24).

I propose deliverance ministers need to become more God conscious than sin conscious. If we operate out of legalism, we will become judgmental and possibly even a little self-righteous. Am I right? But God consciousness is a paradigm wherein we are focused on Him. *"Looking unto Jesus, the author and finisher of our faith..."* (Hebrews 12:2). What is Jesus saying in this situation? What is Jesus doing? What is the Holy Spirit revealing? We must remember that mercy always triumphs over judgment (James 2:13).

If someone is having an issue with sin, humbly and gently correct them in love. I like to imagine the apostle Paul, with his weathered skin and dark curly hair, coaching his protégé Timothy on this topic. He said, *"A servant of the LORD must not quarrel but be gentle to all, able to teach, patient, in humility correcting those who are in opposition, if God perhaps will grant them repentance, so that they may know the truth, and that they may come to their senses and escape the snare of the devil, having been taken captive by him to do his will."*

If a ministry recipient trusts and respects the person ministering to them, they are more likely to heed Biblical instruction and transition into repentance by the power of the Holy Spirit. Rather than condemning a failure, ask discovery questions to find the root of the wounding that produced the behavior. "What were you feeling?" or "What was happening inside at that moment?"

Do not use scripture to judge or condemn anyone. Instead speak of love, forgiveness, and the power of grace to overcome. If a need for repentance is indicated, you can ask the ministry recipient, "What is the Holy Spirit saying to you about this behavior?" If they can hear the LORD, this is the most effective method. Certainly, if the gentle approach doesn't work, you may have to be more direct to encourage repentance, but be careful not to shame or threaten.

SPIRITUAL ABUSE

Any discussion on ministry wounding would be incomplete without the mention of spiritual abuse. This is a very important consideration for ministers. People see ministers as authority figures. It is important not to misuse this authority (See Matthew 20:25-28). Ministers should never shame, threaten, coerce, manipulate, dominate or intimidate the people to whom they minister. The minister should never tell the person they are serving to keep secrets or maintain silence. And emotional care should always preclude deliverance; people before demons.

Permit me to tell you another story. Last year, I was sitting in a meeting of deliverance ministers from all over the world. A renowned speaker was teaching on basic deliverance. In her teaching, the speaker described ministering to a woman with a spirit of fear. The speaker determined that the spirit of fear had come in when the woman in her care was two years old. She boldly proclaimed, "I told her to REPENT for that spirit of fear and cast it out of her."

The entire room of ministers laughed, but it wasn't funny. What could have happened to a two-year-old child that would cause a spirit of fear to come in? Did a two-year-old sin because she was scared, and therefore needed to repent? A child can no more control feeling frightened than they can control getting hungry, thirsty or bedwetting at two-years of age. What I heard was pride in authority, and what she described was taking her great big deliverance sword and stuffing it right into that wound. It is shaming to insist a person repent for something they have no control over. It is emotional and spiritual abuse, an endemic problem in the Church today.

What could have been done differently? I suggest that we minister love first, before casting out spirits. Care for the child, minister to the wound, then cast out the spirit. Once the wounding is healed, there is no place in the soul for the spirit to attach, and the spirit can be evicted with a whispered command. Too often the wounding isn't addressed, and the spirit simply returns, because wounds attract infection.

Jesus embodied His authority, He didn't strut around like a rooster with a badge on His chest. No, His authority was implicit and recognized by the enemy. As ministers of Christ, our authority is too. We must always be on guard to ensure we are not perpetrating spiritual abuse. To follow are some commonly recognized signs of spiritual abuse.

1. Someone who 'hears God' on your behalf and insists you heed the 'word' at your peril.
2. 'LORD's over' others in power/authority and limits free will or alternative viewpoints.
3. Exclusionary, "you are either for me or against me," fosters "us versus them," mentality.
4. Inclusionary, rewards obedience with praise and perks.
5. Uses confidential or secret information as a tool for control or compliance.
6. Uses manipulation, silent treatment and/or threats of rejection to control others.
7. Insists their position, leadership or revelatory knowledge provides them special rights.
8. Shames and blames others for behaviors outside of their control.
9. Yells, mocks, humiliates, or chides others for what they believe.
10. Uses scripture in a harmful manner: inducing legalism, guilt, judgment or shame.

11. Attempts to cast out a dissociative identity, treating the identity as a demon.

Peter wrote: *"Shepherd the flock of God which is among you, serving as overseers, not by compulsion but willingly, not for dishonest gain but eagerly; nor as being Lord's over those entrusted to you, but being examples to the flock; and when the Chief Shepherd appears, you will receive the crown of glory that does not fade away"* (1 Peter 5:2-4).

RESPONDING TO PAIN

This may be a good juncture to insert my belief that a born again Christian, on fire with the Holy Spirit, doesn't have to be ordained to be a minister. As members of the Body of Christ, we are all called to love and care for one another, bearing each other's burdens (Gal. 6:2). But sometimes we are clumsy and just don't know how to respond to people in pain. To follow is an example of what not to do with your friends or ministry recipients.

Many years ago, I was invited to lunch by a Christian co-worker during a particularly difficult time in my life. I was a working mom with a very stressful job, running three departments. My marriage was rocky and I was grappling with horrific childhood memories of near death experiences, while also suffering with bulimia. Grateful for the invitation to get out of the office, I met my co-worker at a nearby restaurant. Once we were seated, she gave me a huge smile and said, "You need to smile more. Just be happy!" Her face lit up, she took a deep breath and sang right there in the restaurant, "You've got the joy, joy, joy, joy down in your heart..." complete with hand gestures.

If you could have seen my face, I was completely jaw dropping mortified. It deeply hurt my feelings. Although I quickly forgave her, that was the last lunch we had together. What happened there? She had an agenda to "correct me", presumably because I was not a happy camper at work. She didn't ask me what was happening in my life or why I was so sad. Instead, she completely invalidated my feelings, and I felt thoroughly judged. I didn't feel happy, but she was telling me as a Christian it was my duty to feel something I didn't. How common is this in the Body of Christ? How many hurting people have experienced this same scenario from well-meaning friends and family? It breaks my heart to think it is commonplace. Proper emotional care acknowledges feelings, without denying them or trying to change them. A loving Christian response to pain is to listen and to pray for comfort and healing. If you have ever struggled to know what to say to people who are suffering, the next chapter offers some suggestions.

Proverbs 25:20 says it best, *"Like one who takes off a garment on a cold day, or like vinegar on soda, is he who sings songs to a troubled heart."*

CHAPTER 6

MINISTRY TO THE HEAVY HEART

An experienced and well-respected minister responded to my concerns about emotional care in ministry by telling me emotional care is only applicable to the deeply traumatized, such as ritual abuse survivors. But that's not true. Everyone has feelings. Throughout the seasons in a person's life, there will be times when everyone will experience a heavy heart. To effectively minister, we need to master a few skills such as creating emotional safety, building trust, purposeful listening, and the validation of feelings. And there are a few things not to do, like trying to fix apparent problems, giving unsolicited advice or responding with judgment or criticism. Ultimately, the objective is to provide a safe place for people to unload the burdens in their heart. After doing so, most people will tell you they feel better. These skills can be applied in all your relationships, especially with family members because the best ministry starts at home.

EMOTIONAL SAFETY

You may be wondering, what is emotional safety? Psychologists have a variety of definitions, but for our purposes, emotional safety can simply be defined as a state where people feel safe to share deeply from their heart without fear of emotional harm. Safety in the ministry relationship is critical to the healing process. Minister's that genuinely seek the safety of their ministry recipients will find their effectiveness accelerate exponentially. For some people, the ministry relationship may be the only safe place to heal, grow, and make mistakes. This is the power of love in action.

When Isaiah prophesied about the coming Messiah he wrote, *"A bruised reed He will not break, and smoking flax He will not quench"* (Isaiah 42:3). The smoking flax is a picture of a lamp wick that is ready to be snuffed out. But our Savior will not quench the remaining flames of hope in our hearts. He tenderly nourishes and cares for us. He breathes new life into the embers of our dreams. As His representatives, we can do no less for others.

Emotional safety creates an environment for trust to develop and the heart to open. It is also a subject where ministers seem to need the most coaching. To create this safety a person needs assurance that the listener will protect confidentiality and not gossip about them. People need to feel they are in a "judgment free zone," where there is an umbrella sense of respect for their personal dignity. There can be no shaming, no hint of rejection or criticism, just a prevailing sense of love and care.

People need their ministers to be authentic, genuine and transparent. A minister's carefully constructed façade will not withstand the survival skills of a person that has been traumatized. They will see right through them and it will be harder to earn their trust.

BODY LANGUAGE

Believe it or not, body language goes a long way in establishing trust. People read nonverbal cues. If the look on your face matches the words you are saying, there is a sense of congruence. For example, if I tell you I'm listening, but I'm staring at my cell phone, that's a problem. If my arms are crossed in a defensive position, the person I am with may feel guarded too. But if I look at ease and feel at ease, this will translate also. To communicate active listening, body language is very important. Look the person in the eye, put down what you are holding, and lean forward in your chair. This body language conveys the message, "I'm engaged in what you are saying and I care."

LISTENING SKILLS

Listening skills are paramount to effectiveness. How do we listen well? We listen by being fully engaged in what the other person is saying. We don't interrupt. We pay attention to our senses and become observant. Is there emotion in the voice tone? Is the verbiage coming out fast, high pitched, or rhythmic? What isn't being said? What is the other person's body language saying?

There are really two parts to listening skills. The first is hearing. The second is communicating in such a manner as the person feels heard. This is called "reflective listening." As with any skill, listening skills can be developed.

My favorite quote on effective listening skills is from Dr. Stephen Covey who said, "Seek first to understand, then to be understood." In his wildly successful book "7 Habits of Highly Effective People" he wrote:

> If you're like most people, you probably seek first to be understood; you want to get your point across. And in doing so, you may ignore the other person completely, pretend that you're listening, selectively hear only certain parts of the conversation or attentively focus on only the words being said, but miss the meaning entirely. So why does this happen? Because most people listen with the intent to reply, not to understand. You listen to yourself as you prepare in your mind what you are going to say, the questions you are going to ask, etc. You filter everything you hear through your life experiences, your frame of reference. You

check what you hear against your autobiography and see how it measures up. And consequently, you decide prematurely what the other person means before he/she finishes communicating.

Recently a friend called me to share her heavy heart. She had just discovered her mother was dying of cancer. Her biggest concern was that her mother wasn't saved and she wanted to share the gospel with her. I suggested she seek first to understand her mother's heart. I said, "Take her hand and look her in the eyes. Just ask her how she feels about what's happening to her. People don't usually know what to say to someone dying and the subject is rarely brought up. But she probably needs to share her feelings about death. After she shares her heart, you can share yours with her. She may be more open to hearing the gospel at that point."

Reflective listening is an important skill to develop. It is simply the act of reflecting back to the speaker what was heard and observed by paraphrasing what was said or noting an emotion. For example, "I heard you say ___." Then you can ask a question to expand on the topic. "How do you feel about what happened?"

One could say, "That sounds very painful," or "I can sense your anger." You can even say, "I noticed when you said ___, I observed ___." When the speaker hears the reflection back from the listener they know they have been heard.

Over the years my husband has become a very skilled listener. He knows me so well; he can tell when I need to vent. He may encourage me to come join him on the couch or he may invite me out for dinner. When I'm really having a tough day, he suggests we take a long drive in the country. He knows within a few minutes I'll unload my heart. Sometimes he will even comment, "I know, this is the part where I'm not supposed to give you my feedback." Or when I'm really upset he may say, "I don't have to fix this right?"

His loving care for me in these ways makes me love him more.

To further develop your listening skills, you might try an online tutorial or take a self-test or two. Your family and friends will love you for it and you might just become the busiest minister in town.

EMOTIONAL HARM

The next important aspect to communication in ministry is to ensure we don't cause emotional harm with the things we say in response to a heavy heart. Emotional harm occurs when a person discounts, denies, or minimizes the feelings of others. Here are some examples: "Oh, it's not that bad!" or "You don't really feel that way, do you?" or how about, "You need to just pull yourself up by your bootstraps and move on."

Shaming occurs when things are said like, "If you had more faith..." or "shame on you, you should know better than to..." or "If you had listened to what I said in the first place..."

The truth is, when people are wounded, they can get stuck emotionally. The new wineskin provides for safe emotional processing, so people can move on. Love says, "I hear you."

VALIDATION

People often experience a sense that their feelings are wrong or that they shouldn't feel the way they do. In Western culture, where feelings are second class citizens, validation goes a long way in comforting a heavy heart. Validation is simply acknowledging the importance of a person's feelings; like the balm of Gilead. In most cases, it's appropriate to say, "If I were in this situation, I would feel the same way." By conveying the message that a person's feelings are normal, a minister can build trust, safety, and facilitate healing.

STOP TRYING TO FIX IT!

One of the most tempting things to do when a person hears the plight of another, is to attempt to fix the problem. This is called rescuing. It is an unhealthy dynamic in relationships. The truth is we can't be someone else's savior or fix their problems without creating more problems. Instead, it is wise to ask questions, direct them to the voice of the Holy Spirit or facilitate an encounter with Jesus. Ask, "If you could hear God speaking to you right now, what would He say?" I asked this question to a person that was unsaved recently and to my astonishment she heard God immediately speak to her heart. I knew it was God because what she shared could only have come from divine inspiration.

UNSOLICITED ADVICE

Another temptation to avoid is the idea that people want your advice because they are sharing their problems with you. No. Most people don't want advice, they need freedom to express their emotions, it can be like air to breathe. I've made this mistake with my youngest son. He is a talented artist trying to make his way in the world. And I, with my business degree and wealth of experience, thought I could help him with my savvy advice. One evening I pummeled him with things to do to make his mark on the world, and it made him feel terrible. After that, he was reluctant to discuss his ideas with me, and I realized I hurt his heart.

If you are looking for a way to share an idea you can always frame it in the form of a question, "Have you considered ...?" or "Would you like some feedback?" This gives people the opportunity to choose for themselves and it is respectful.

REFRAIN FROM JUDGMENT

Jesus warned us, *"Judge not, that you be not judged. For with what judgment you judge, you will be judged; and with the measure you use, it will be measured back to you"* (Matt. 7:1-2).

Often people don't realize others experience them as judgmental. But people can intuitively sense a critical, judgmental, or condescending attitude in others. Conversely, they can also sense being accepted and loved. To follow is an example illustrating this point.

I was at my adult daughter's birthday party recently and I had the opportunity to join a small group of women for their discussion in the kitchen. One was a long-distance runner like me, so I enjoyed asking about her training schedule and advice for running my first marathon. The other two ladies were married to each other and had a beautiful little girl. They were aware that I am a pastor so they were cautious with their conversation around me, sniffing the proverbial air for any hint of my judgment. I just listened as they talked about the challenges they face and some of the heartache they feel. When the evening was over, I hugged each of the ladies and went home with my husband.

A few days later my daughter called and said, "Thanks, mom."

"For what?" I replied.

She said, "My friend wanted me to pass along her thanks to you for listening to her at the party. Her mom won't speak to her anymore. Just the fact that you listened really meant a lot to her."

If I had been more sin conscious than God conscious, I would have hurt this woman in my judgment by walking away rather than hearing her heart. But mercy opened a doorway to love that may someday open more doorways of conversation.

I live in the Pacific Northwest where homosexuality is commonplace. Most of the people I have encountered that identify themselves this way expect to be harshly judged by Christians. As a result, Christians are known for our judgment, not our love. And Christians are reaping the fruit of that judgment right back. The problem is as Christians we are seeing a behavior that is identified in the Scripture as a sin, but neglecting the weightier matter of a people that are hurting. *"For all have sinned and fall short of the glory of God"* (Romans 3:23). How can we reach people with the love of Christ if they rightfully come to expect we will hurt them?

In my work with severe trauma survivors, each time, I have encountered a person that is struggling with homosexuality it is the result of sexual abuse and/or deep emotional wounding. When people can trust me to love them unconditionally they are able to open their heart and share their deepest heartache and shame. Once these things come to the light God's healing can be made manifest. Let's express the mercy of Christ with the brokenhearted and discover the indescribable healing power of love.

Paul gave exceptional pastoral counseling advice in Romans 12:15. He said, *"Rejoice with those who rejoice, and weep with those who weep."*

If you are looking for an additional resource on this topic, I suggest getting a copy of the book, "Don't Sing Songs to a Heavy Heart; How to Relate to Those Who Are Suffering" by Kenneth C. Haugk. For sexual healing resources, I recommend materials from David Kyle Foster at Mastering Life Ministries. http://purepassion.us.

"Blessed be the God and Father of our LORD Jesus Christ, the Father of mercies and God of all comfort, who comforts us in all our tribulation, that we may be able to comfort those who are in any trouble, with the comfort with which we ourselves are comforted by God. For as the sufferings of Christ abound in us, so our consolation also abounds through Christ"

(2 Cor. 2:3-5).

CHAPTER 7

JUDGMENT

The word "judgment" is power packed. When used in court, it carries a sense of weighty finality. When it comes to emotional matters, it's in a class of its own. Heavy and unyielding, judgments tend to get in the way of healthy relationships. To judge is to form an opinion and we all have opinions. But judgment often follows with criticism, both are attitudes that can make it feel unsafe for people to express themselves. Without emotional safety in ministry people don't heal on the very deep levels necessary to restore their lives.

MORAL JUDGMENT ON BEHAVIOR

As Christians, we are called upon to discern moral right and wrong and to uphold Biblical standards of righteousness in our conduct. We are instructed to judge behavior. As Paul said, *"Do you not know that we shall judge angels? How much more, things that pertain to this life?"* (1 Corinthians 6:3).

Other examples of this can be found in the Old Testament book of Judges, written about a thousand years before Christ was born. The text details how the Israelites sinned by doing evil in the sight of the LORD and were oppressed by their enemies. When the Israelites cried out for deliverance, God gave them judges. Much like our judges today, their job was to determine moral right from wrong and lead the people in the way they should go. They were leaders who provided wise counsel and restored righteousness in the community. My favorite of these Old Testament judges is Deborah. She was a prophetess, a war strategist, and a mother to Israel. In a modern context, she would be the equivalent of the first female Supreme Court judge who led a nation to victory in battle, without a single sword or spear (Judges 5:8).

The ability to properly discern right from wrong is critical to effectiveness in everyday matters; from religion, to parenting, from employment to politics, healthcare to education, and military might. Good moral judgment prevents apostasy, which was rampant during the time of the book of Judges and is rampant in our culture today. Isaiah issued this warning, *"Woe to those who call evil good, and good evil"* (Isaiah 5:20).

UNRIGHTEOUS JUDGMENT OF CHARACTER AND IDENTITY

In contrast to the moral judgment of behavior, we are not called upon to judge the character and identity of people. Jesus said, *"Judge not, that you be not judged; for with what judgment you judge, you will be judged; and with the measure you use, it will be measured back to you"* (Matthew 7:1-2). There is a spiritual principle of sowing and reaping involved with judging people.

To say it another way, we are to judge the sin and not the sinner. But how do we know where to draw that line? It's the difference between behavior and identity. Picture the concept by looking at both hands, behavior and identity. They are two different things. I may do something wrong, which is my behavior (left hand), but it doesn't change who I am in Christ (right hand). If I run a red light that is wrong and may come with consequences. But it doesn't make me unredeemable.

To render a good judgment, people need good facts. In the same way, the judge in a courtroom reviews evidence before deciding upon a verdict. As human beings, we could never have enough information to rightly judge the character of another person. God is the only infallible judge. He is merciful and gracious. He sees the beginning from the end. He knows His own creation.

When we judge people, we are rendering an opinion. The question is whether our opinions become destructive forces that wound people and hinder our ability to experience them as they really are; as God sees them. When we judge other people, in a sense, we are playing God, and it is not likely we are seeing them as He does.

Jesus said, *"And why do you look at the speck in your brother's eye, but do not consider the plank in your own eye?"* (Matthew 7:3). He continued in verse 5, *"Hypocrite! First remove the plank from your own eye, and then you will see clearly to remove the speck from your brother's eye."*

Paul has this to say about it in Romans 2:1, *"Therefore you are inexcusable, O man, whoever you are who judge, for in whatever you judge another you condemn yourself; for you who judge practice the same things."* Ouch! Paul doesn't mince words here in verse 3! *"And do you think this, O man, you who judge those practicing such things, and doing the same, that you will escape the judgment of God?"*

As much as I'd like to think I am not judgmental, surely, I deceive myself. As a deliverance minister, I have good spiritual discernment and a keen sense of moral right and wrong. Over the years I have noticed people with good discernment are likely to be the most judgmental, it's certainly true for me. It's easy to blur the line between someone's behavior and their character as a person. While leading people into repentance for their deliverance in ministry, I can become overly sin focused rather than God conscious. And it's easy to see things in others that I don't like to see in myself. Paul said, *"Who are you to judge another's servant? To his own master he stands or falls"* (Romans 14:4).

This is important for two reasons. First, people are being wounded in churches and ministries that are operating out of judgment rather than love and tender mercy. James 2:13 says, *"For judgment is without mercy to the one who has shown no mercy. Mercy triumphs over judgment."*

When God brings in the harvest, if we judge people rather than embrace them, they may never reach out again. Let's not be like the Pharisees, hypocrites that would travel land and sea for one (Matthew 23:15), and reject a thousand others hungry for Christ. Jesus told us not to judge according to appearance, but righteously (John 7:24).

The second important reason to address the matter of unrighteous judgment (judgment of another's identity and character), is that it causes bondage to the judge and defilement for others.

BITTER ROOT JUDGMENTS

John and Paula Sandford of Elijah House Ministries (www. elijahhouse.org) developed an amazing teaching years ago on bitter root judgments. In their work, they unpacked this with scriptures and amazing revelation. Hebrews 12:14 & 15 Amplified version reads, *"Strive to live in peace with everybody and pursue that consecration and holiness without which no one will [ever] see the LORD. Exercise foresight and be on the watch to look [after one another] to see that no one falls back from and fails to secure God's grace (His unmerited favor and spiritual blessing) in order that no root of resentment (rancor, bitterness or hatred) shoots forth and causes trouble and bitter torment, and the many become contaminated and defiled by it."*

Bitter root judgments are judgments that cause a bitter root to develop in the heart and they set several spiritual principles in motion.

1. It binds the judge and the person judged together with cords of unrighteousness. The judge, acting as god, separates from God. Therefore, the LORD isn't in the circumstance to redeem the situation.
2. The sowing of judgments causes a reaping effect that may replicate repeatedly in a person's life.
3. From the seed of judgment grows a root of bitterness in the heart that pulls from bitter waters. Those bitter waters can breed disease and emotional drama.
4. The reaping of a bitter root judgment can defile many people.

For example, a lady came into my office complaining about her neighbor. They had been friends, but she rejected her and refused to speak with her again. I asked her why she thought this may have happened. She said, "I don't know, but this has happened so many times in my life. It happened with my husband, my pastor, my father and my best friend."

I asked her to tell me about the first time it occurred. She told me she was twelve when her father stopped being affectionate with her, and their relationship was never the same. "He never even said a word about it, he just stopped loving me!" she cried.

I asked her, "What happens to little girls when they are about twelve?" She shook her head, "I don't know."

I suggested, "They develop and become women. Could your father have felt uncomfortable being so affectionate with you when he realized you were developing into a woman?"

She admitted she had never considered that idea. But she did harshly judge her father for suddenly withholding affection and never saying a word. This scenario replicated five times in her life before she addressed it with me. The judgment could have been defined as, "Dad is mean, he rejected me and never said a word as to why." Whenever, I see a repeating scenario in ministry, I suspect bitter root judgments.

How does a person know they are holding a bitter root judgment? One of the best ways I've found is to ask the Holy Spirit to reveal them for each primary relationship in a person's life. This would include parents, spouses, family members, friends, teachers, and people in authority. Abuse survivors would do well to check for judgments against perpetrators. Finally, it is important to consider a list of judgments held against self and against God. Sometimes these are the most revealing.

Take a sheet of blank paper and write at the top "I feel ___ (person) is ___ " (fill in the blank). Finish this sentence with the words that immediately come to mind. Don't censor or analyze the information, just let it flow onto the paper as a right-brained exercise.

When the Holy Spirit began addressing bitter root judgments in my life, I started with my husband. I think I had two pages of content. One of the items on the list was the word "stubborn." I'm a pioneer and my husband is a settler. We lived in our first house for seventeen years, it took me five years to get him to sell it. I protested to the Holy Spirit, "I'm not just making this up, he really is stubborn!" Then Holy Spirit shared with me the character quality He had placed in my husband. "In judgment, this characteristic looks like stubbornness, but in mercy, it is the quality of being steadfast."

"Oh," I thought, "I can see that." Then He continued, "I gave you a steadfast husband because you needed one. If it had been up to you, you would have dragged your children from one end of the country to the other. I wanted them to have stability growing up so I gave you the gift of a man that is steadfast."

God is so merciful in His correction which leads to repentance. From that point forward Ryan ceased to be stubborn in my eyes and our relationship improved. My judgment had precluded my ability to see my husband as the LORD saw him and to value the gift within him.

We do not sin in a vacuum. If we judge, we reap that same judgment and it can affect all of those around us. What if a pastor judged a member of his congregation for adultery? Agreeably, adultery is morally wrong. But if the pastor judges the character of another person, he is in danger of sowing a seed of adultery. If the pastor falls into the sin of adultery himself, he has reaped what he has sown and the entire congregation, his family, and the person with whom he sinned are all affected! By this many can be defiled.

Rick Joyner wrote in "There Were Two Trees in the Garden" page 154, "We must stop casting stones at others who fall short of God's glory because we have also fallen. When we judge another servant or congregation of the LORD, *we are in fact judging Him.* When we judge one of God's children we are in effect saying that His workmanship does not meet up to our standards and that we could do better."

Those with a gift of discernment often have very long lists! When this gift operates in the flesh it can produce judgment. When discernment operates in the Spirit it produces life and revelation.

After generating a list of judgments, they can be broken with these steps.

1. Repent for judging others and for judging God.
2. Forgive liberally.
3. Ask the Holy Spirit to show you the condition of your heart.

4. Pray: "In the Name of Jesus, I break the bitter root judgments I have held against _____ "
   a. List the names of the people.
   b. List the judgments.
5. Break the judgments under the blood of Jesus, at the sowing and at the reaping.
6. Ask the LORD to burn that harvest crop of bad fruit.
7. Bind and cast out the demonic spirits on each of the judgments.
8. Pray a blessing on those judged.
9. Ask the Holy Spirit to help you see each person as He sees them.

Discovering the judgments in your own heart and working through them will enable you to learn how to walk free of judgment. It takes time, diligence, and obedience to the prompting of the Holy Spirit. But we can learn new ways of relating more effectively.

MERCY VS JUDGMENT

"Baker's Evangelical Dictionary of Biblical Theology" has this to say about Mercy:

> Mercy is a concept integral to an understanding of God's dealings with humankind. In English translations of the Bible, it comes to expression in phrases such as "to be merciful, " "to have mercy on," or "to show mercy toward." The corresponding term, "merciful," describes a quality of God and one that God requires of his people. The noun denotes compassion and love, not just feelings or emotions, as expressed in tangible ways.[8]

---

8   http://www.biblestudytools.com/dictionary/mercy/ 8.12.17

Extending mercy is like extending a life preserver to a drowning man. Emotionally, mercy creates safety, as a tangible expression of love. Mercy is associated with the Spirit and the love of God, while judgment is associated with the law. *"But now we have been delivered from the law, having died to what we were held by, so that we should serve in the newness of the Spirit and not in the oldness of the letter"* (Romans 7:6).

Repeatedly God said in His word, *"I desire mercy and not sacrifice"* (Hosea 6:6, Matt. 9:13 and Matt. 12:7). I believe God is calling us to extend tender loving-kindness to one another and not the judgment that comes with an infraction of the law. When Jesus said these words to the Pharisees He was making it clear that loving people was more important than the blood of lambs or bulls (Hosea 6:6). This truth is applicable as much today as it was then. If we are to be a people that minister as Jesus did, like Jesus with skin on, we must remember He didn't come to judge the world, but to save it (John 13:47).

CHAPTER 8

HUMILITY; A MATTER OF IDENTITY

"What makes humility so desirable is the marvelous thing it does to us; it creates in us a capacity for the closest possible intimacy with God"

– Monica Baldwin

If we really want to be effective for Christ in this world, we need to learn how to love, and we must be humble, or we will hurt the people the LORD has entrusted us to serve. Humility is often misunderstood, and generally undervalued, but permit me to share my thoughts.

It's common knowledge that Jesus made his debut in the world, in a lowly manger. But it wasn't the manger that defined Him. He was about His Father's business by the age of twelve, but it wasn't His knowledge of the scripture or his ability to teach in the synagogue that defined Him. He worked as a carpenter, but even as a Master Craftsman, his skill did not define Him. The fulfillment of ancient prophecies about Jesus didn't even define Him. At thirty years old, it was His Heavenly Father that gave Jesus His identity when he declared, *"You are My Beloved Son; in You I am well pleased"* (Luke 3:22).

True humility is a matter of walking in our identity as sons and daughters of the living God. We come to the Father through His Son. And at the foot of the cross, all human beings are equal. Shoulder to shoulder, no one is worth more, and no one is worth less.

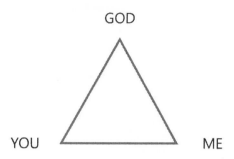

In the presence of God, we are humbled. We may gasp like Isaiah, *"I'm undone!"* (Isaiah 6:5). In an instant, we know we are not God, yet loved by God immeasurably. We are fully accepted in the Beloved (Ephesians 1:6), so there is no fear of rejection. There is no need for sibling rivalry, jealousy or competition; because our Heavenly Father loves each one of us equally and there are plenty of good gifts to go around. All we need to do is ask, and we shall receive (Luke 11:9).

If our identity is not fully formed in our Heavenly Father, then we are likely to find our sense of self in our accomplishments, skills, gifting, or even the needs of others. Without a proper identity, we may rely on the opinions of others to define who we are, and we will be swayed by the opinions of man, rather than the leading of the Holy Spirit and the Word of God. The devil knows this will leave us vulnerable to temptation.

PRIDE AND FALSE HUMILITY

When I first began ministering, I was astounded by the anointing of God. People lined-up for prayer and the gifts of the Holy Spirit flowed like cisterns of living water. The experience was absolutely exhilarating! And pride thoroughly tempted me. For ten days in a row, I got on my face before God and repented for pride, until the temptation subsided. Ten is the number of testing.

I confessed my struggle to my mentor George. He reminded me that God could use a doorknob or a donkey to get His point across, but He chose to use me. I wasn't sure whether to be flattered or offended, two sides of the same coin; pride and false humility. Both are falsehoods. No one is less than, no one is more than, God shows no partiality (Romans 2:11). Roles may indicate hierarchy, but when it comes to identity, God wants us to know that we are all on a level field. Shoulder to shoulder, I'm no better than you, I'm not less than you. I get to be me! Even if I make a mistake, I am not a mistake. I'm still me. I'm a beloved child of God. You can't change that!

Flattery isn't real. It's just a manipulation that appeals to the desire to be "better than." Pride puffs up, and like a balloon, it's just hot air. There's nothing of genuine substance about it.

In my service to the LORD, I have met many ministers from all walks of life, all over the world. One thing I find most unbecoming of a Christian minister is pride. The danger with pride is it comes with blindness. We may not even realize we are operating in pride. Therefore, it is wisdom to have two or three trusted, God fearing, individuals in our lives that have been given permission to speak to any evidence of pride or false humility in us.

The apostle Paul said, *"Knowledge puffs up, but love edifies. And if anyone thinks that he knows anything, he knows nothing yet as he ought to know"* (1 Corinthians 8:1-2).

"Not that we are sufficient of ourselves to think of anything as being from ourselves, but our sufficiency is from God, who also made us sufficient as ministers of the new covenant, not of the letter but of the Spirit; for the letter kills, but the Spirit gives life" (2 Corinthians 3:5-6).

We must remember we are each part of the body of Christ. He never intended for one person, or one ministry to have all the answers, or we wouldn't be dependent on Him or work together.

Jesus didn't serve others because it made Him feel better about Himself. He didn't need a big "calling" to bolster His self-esteem. Humbly Jesus said, *"...the Son can do nothing of Himself, but what He sees the Father do; for whatever He does, the Son also does in like manner"* (John 5:19).

SELF-RELIANCE

As ministers, we need to stay so connected to the Vine, that self-reliance and independence are abhorrent to our spirit. Instead, in this modern world of instant gratification, we must learn to wait on Him, and only do what we see the Father doing. If we succumb to the temptation to become the source of our own effectiveness, pride will surely set in. *"Pride goes before destruction, and a haughty spirit before a fall"* (Proverbs 16:18).

Several years ago, I was struggling with severe exhaustion in the ministry. I brought the matter before the LORD one morning in prayer. The Holy Spirit gently spoke to my heart, noting that I had not spent much time alone with Him lately. I was busy "doing" but had long since been serving in my own strength. He reminded me of a dream that illustrated this point. In the dream, I was peddling a bicycle on a bumpy dirt road. I was getting very tired peddling, and frustrated with my lack of progress. It seemed I wasn't getting anywhere despite my greatest effort. The LORD began to speak to my spirit and I understood that the bicycle in the dream was self-propelled, the reason for my exhaustion. I realized by operating in self-will, by self-propulsion, I was operating in pride and self-reliance, independent of God. Psalm 10:4 says, *"The wicked in his proud countenance does not seek God."*

I didn't know exactly when it happened, but I found myself walking in the flesh rather than in the Spirit. God designed me as an administrator; it seems I always have a pad of paper and a task list handy. I tend to perceive my own value based upon what I can accomplish in a day. That performance identity has been the focus of many conversations with the LORD over the years. One thing I have learned, Sabbath rest is the paradox wherein the greatest things of heaven's kingdom are accomplished.

TRUSTING GOD

Walking in the Spirit, in full humility, is about surrender and trust; two things with which the wounded soul may wrestle. Trust in God is required to walk in humility, otherwise, we will take matters into our own hands and risk becoming self-reliant and prideful. The LORD knew I struggled in this area and He said to me once, "Katie, I will do whatever it takes to earn your trust because I love you." He has never failed me, regardless of the circumstances.

REJECTION

Many people enter ministry as they overcome the challenges of their own past. It's so important that ministers attend to their own rejection wounds and overcome the victim mentality and the orphan spirit before attempting to serve someone else. Identity must be grounded in sonship or people can easily become offended, fearful, defensive and angry. They may even attempt to build their own little kingdom, rather than becoming a partner in His.

The spirit of rejection attempts to separate us from our primary relationships: God, others, and self. In so doing, we deny the greatest commandment. The deception at the root of this lie is that God could/would reject us. But the truth is nothing can separate us from the love of God (Romans 8:38-39).

SHAME AND SELF-DEPRECATION

There was a time when I thought the antidote to pride was self-deprecation, but nothing could be further from the truth. Self-abasement is false humility. The truth is I am not "less than" anyone else; that's what makes it false. I thought it was an act of humility when I hung my head in shame. But no, God did not give me an identity of shame. He gave me an identity as His child, fashioned in His image. When I denied my identity in Christ, I denied His craftsmanship. It was like saying to the world's greatest artist, "that painting isn't very good."

I recall listening to an audio teaching on shame by Joyce Meyer many years ago. In it, she described a shame-based personality. Immediately I thought, "That's me!" I'm always looking for approval, I'm always saying "I'm sorry" and I feel intrinsically flawed. It is this shame-base in the foundation of the soul that says, "There's something wrong with me." It is the basis for the double-sided coin of false humility and pride.

In her teaching, Joyce Meyer suggested people pray for God to remove the shame foundation. Wholeheartedly, I prayed into the matter. God is so faithful. It didn't happen instantly, but progressively over the years, He provided new tools, and revelation to restore me at the very core of my identity. He said, "Are you going to believe what the world says about you, or what the enemy says about you? Or will you believe what I say about you in My Word?"

SCRIPTURAL IDENTITY

The LORD instructed me to take a list of identity scriptures and stand in front of a mirror and speak them out loud, daily, until I believed what He said. The following are a few examples:

- I am a saint (Eph. 1:1; 1 Cor. 1:2; Phil. 1:1; Col. 1:2).
- I am a child of God (John 1:12).
- I am the light of the world (Matt. 5:14).
- I am the salt of the earth (Matt. 5:13).
- I am Christ's friend (John 15:15).
- I am chosen & appointed to bear good fruit, and the fruit shall remain (John 15:16).
- I am chosen of God, holy and dearly loved (Col. 3:12).
- I am righteous and holy (Eph. 4:24).
- I have been given the mind of Christ (1 Cor. 2:16).
- I am a new creation (2 Cor. 5:17).
- I am a holy temple (1 Cor. 3:16; 6:19).

Each scripture is rich in meaning, almost overwhelming to comprehend. So, I took my favorite from the list and meditated on that one, *"I am chosen & appointed to bear good fruit"* (John 15:16).

I am chosen. Those words rolled around in my heart powerfully. Like a wrecking ball, they battered the walls of rejection inside of me until they crumbled. God chose me!

I have been appointed to bear good fruit. The God of the entire universe determined beforehand that I would bear good fruit. I thought of Jesus' words in Matthew 7:17, *"Even so, every healthy (sound) tree bears good fruit [worthy of admiration] ..."* (AMP). The fig tree produces figs, the apple tree produces apples. I wondered, "What kind of fruit do I produce?" A picture came to mind of a beautiful tree firmly planted along the banks of a mighty river, flowing from the throne of God (Rev. 22:1). I just had to look up this scripture. It continued, "... *on either side of the river was the tree of life with its twelve varieties of fruit, yielding each month its fresh crop; and the leaves of the tree were for the healing and the restoration of the nations*" (Rev. 22:2 AMP).

"What do trees do to bear fruit?" I wondered. I knew they put down firm roots, and draw nourishment from the sun. Ephesians 3:17 came to mind, "*That Christ may dwell in your hearts through faith; that you, <u>being rooted and grounded in love</u>, may be able to comprehend with all the saints what is the width and length and depth and height – to know the love of Christ which passes knowledge; that you may be filled with all the fullness of God.*"

I realized that as a good tree, rooted and grounded in the love of Christ, my roots could draw up living water from the river of the throne of God, and I would bear good fruit in the brilliant light of the Son. When I prayed, I pictured this tree overflowing with fruit. Then I pictured my family members as trees alongside me. This powerful imagery inspired my faith and emotions as it reconstructed my identity and prophetically paved the way for Kingdom fruit to be revealed in my life. This was one of many ways the Holy Spirit worked; there were others.

IDENTITY PRIOR TO CONCEPTION

Possibly the most powerful experience to reshape my identity was an experience when Holy Spirit took me back to a time before conception. Wait. What? Before conception, how is that even scriptural or possible? In Ephesians 1:4 Paul says it this way, "*He chose us in Him before the foundation of the world, that we should be holy and without blame before Him in love, having predestined us to adoption...*"

I wondered, "What was I like, before all of the trauma and abuse?

Who was I before God placed me in my mother's womb?" If I was chosen before the foundation of the world, I must have been created. If I was created, and the Word says specifically, in the image of God (Gen. 1:27), then I reasoned I could ask Him for more revelation.

My prayer was simple, "Heavenly Father, will you show me who you created me to be before I came into this world?" And to my surprise, He did! He gave me an image of His enormous hand, with me in the center of His palm, a pure spiritual light. I could see that I was made in His image, a spiritual being. Then I was struck with an epiphany, *"There is nothing intrinsically wrong with who I am!"*

All my life I believed I was deeply flawed, and both the world and the enemy of my soul, were all too happy to confirm that lie. Why? Because if I really walk in my true identity as defined by God, I could fulfill my calling, and become everything the Father purposed for me. This isn't just true for me; it's true for you too. God has a divine purpose for which He created you.

I love the word pictures David used in Psalm 139:15-16, *"My frame was not hidden from You, when I was made in secret, and skillfully wrought in the lowest parts of the earth. Your eyes saw my substance, being yet unformed."* I'm no theologian, and I am not seminary trained in Hebrew or Greek, but I do believe God wanted me to understand that I was originally created pristine and undefiled in Him. There are still times when I fall into old thought patterns, and when I do, Holy Spirit is an ever-present help, gently guiding me back to the truth.

The way we see self has an enormous impact on everything about our life and relationships. The greater the degree with which we are authentic, the less inclined we will be to Lord over people with pride or shrink back in shame and false humility. We each have a choice.

Pride has no place in the new wineskin for healing and deliverance. Everything we are, every gift He has given us, is all from Him. We can't take credit for His work, or steal His glory. Our job is to acknowledge the privilege to serve and partner with Him, and surrender to His will, His way, and His timing.

SURRENDER TO HIS WAYS

"For My thoughts are not your thoughts, nor are your ways My ways, says the LORD. For as the heavens are higher than the earth, so are My ways higher than your ways, and My thoughts than your thoughts" (Isaiah 55:8-9).

When I minister, I have learned to wait on the LORD for His leading in the session. I may be aware of a dozen things that need to be addressed in prayer. But I surrender that list to Him and ask Him to prioritize it. I look at the screen in my mind's eye, to see what Jesus is doing, and that's what we do.

A wise woman named Janice once told me, "It's God's character, God's nature in us that establishes the wineskin for Christ." She said, "It's not my emotions, it's His emotion moving through me. It's His compassion, His rage at the enemy." Janice surely ministers as Jesus with skin on.

When I am teaching, I may have 400 slides and an antsy audience, but I trust the Holy Spirit with the timing. I completely surrender to Him. More than once my hosts have reminded me I was behind with the teaching materials. But I surrender and trust the Holy Spirit to be our teacher. Guess what? We always get through the material and we always end on time.

Whenever I think of myself partnering with Jesus, I imagine the LORD on the floor playing blocks with me. Are we not toddlers building our structures while Jesus smiles and delights in our participation? *"Whosoever therefore shall humble himself as this little child, the same is greatest in the Kingdom of Heaven"* (Matthew 18:4).

HUMILITY

A sign of humility is the ability to admit mistakes. Humble people don't have to be right all the time. They are teachable and can admit their failings because they know that they are unconditionally loved and their identity is not based on their performance.

Humble people don't need to argue to make their point, because truth speaks for itself. Proverbs 13:10 says, *"By pride comes nothing but strife, but the well-advised is wisdom."*

Shame says, "I am a mistake and I have to hide my faults." A shame based identity is formed from a lack of love and nurturing. The belief system says, "There is something fundamentally wrong with me." To compensate, I must always be right. But shame is not from God. We make mistakes because we are human, not because our identity is flawed. The Holy Spirit wants to heal and restore our true identity as sons and daughters of the Most High God.

If we struggle with pride, we need to spend more time in the LORD's presence, and we need a fresh revelation of who we are in Him. *"God has sent forth the Spirit of His Son into our hearts; let us cry "Abba Father!"* (Galatians 4:6) Abba is the cry of a completely dependent infant.

For your further meditation and blessing, consider these scriptures on humility:

The fear of the LORD is the instruction of wisdom, and before honor is humility.

Proverbs 15:33

With humility and the fear of the LORD come riches and honor and life.

Proverbs 22:4

For thus says the High and Lofty One who inhabits eternity, whose name is Holy: "I dwell in the high and holy place with him who has a contrite and humble spirit, to revive the spirit of the humble, and to revive the heart of the contrite ones."

Isaiah 57:15

CHAPTER 9

SAFELY PROCESSING EMOTIONS

Feelings, those elusive wisps that ebb and flow, they are a mystery to the man or woman determined to operate out of reason and logic. Without the proper care of one's emotions, they can seemingly assert themselves from out of nowhere and wreak havoc at the most inopportune times. If you have ever seen road rage, you know what I mean.

Emotions can well-up inside like water in a double boiler. As life heats up the pressure builds, and if we aren't careful, there can be an explosion. But if we learn to care for our emotional well-being and safely process our feelings we can live an authentic life and manage them well. As they are processed the pressure is released and we can face the next dilemma with more self-control. It is possible to feel anger and maintain sanity.

I'm not suggesting people emote their feelings everywhere, or share them with emotionally unsafe people. Emotionally safe people listen without judgment or criticism. They are trustworthy and don't repeat what is shared privately. There is a place and a time for grappling with deep emotions. The workplace isn't one of them, and neither is the Thanksgiving table. Emotional work can be accomplished with a trusted counselor, minister or friend who knows how to minister to a heavy heart. However, there are times, when others aren't available to meet those deep emotional needs. It's comforting to know Jesus would never leave us or forsake us (Hebrews 13:5). He is an ever-present help in times of trouble (Psalm 46:1). Some of the best emotional work in my life was accomplished alone with Jesus, in my devotional time or out for a run with Him in the sunshine.

How does a person work through emotions with the LORD? We can take an example from David. In the Psalms he wrote, *"When my heart is overwhelmed; lead me to the rock that is higher than I"* (Psalm 61:2). David also encourages us to *"Trust in Him at all times, you people; pour out your heart before Him; God is a refuge for us"* (Psalm 62:8).

During my morning devotions many years ago, I received some counsel from the LORD that changed my marriage. I journaled what I heard the LORD say to me concerning an interaction with my husband the night before. Jesus told me when I expressed anger at my husband, I was operating out of pride, and my behavior was deeply hurting him. The LORD instructed me to come directly to Him with my anger, to work through the emotions with Him first, and then when I could calmly discuss it, approach my husband to problem solve issues. It took a long time for my husband to trust that I wouldn't hurt him with my words in anger when we disagreed on something. But over time, we could work through our problems effectively because we created a safe emotional environment for discussion. Jesus is our Wonderful Counselor (Isaiah 9:6).

EMOTIONAL PROCESSING

The first step in emotional processing is to express feelings. You can pour them out in prayer: write them down, type them out, draw or paint them, put them to music, or just tell a safe person. Just let those feelings pour out.

Next, you can use a right-brain exercise to give them to Jesus because emotions are processed in the right hemisphere of the brain. This can be done by first standing on the scripture in 1 Peter 5:7. I prefer the Amplified version, *"Casting the whole of your care [all your anxieties, all your worries, all your concerns, once and for all] on Him, for He cares for you affectionately and cares about you watchfully."*

Picture a camel in your mind's eye. The camel has a heavy pack, and it is kneeling to the ground, so the burden can be rolled off. That's what it means to cast your cares, to let them roll off. Kneeling is a good posture for us too. Sometimes I like to picture myself with a backpack full of rocks. I take the backpack off and hand each rock to Jesus. "This one is my resentment, this one is bitterness, this one is unforgiveness, and Jesus here is my hurt, it's the biggest one."

When I minister to people with big feelings, I ask them, "If the feeling was an object, what would it be?"

People often respond with an object that symbolizes their feelings, such as a knife or an icicle, or even a rock. Sometimes there is quite a story associated with the symbol. Other common symbols are volcanoes, oceans, mountains, etc. You get the idea. Once an object is defined, then picture giving it to Jesus. If imagining Jesus is too scary, an alternative is to leave the object at the foot of the cross or release it to a godly angel. Remember, pictures are the language of the emotions. If we can picture the transfer, our emotions will respond positively.

With major life issues, there can be many layers to the onion. Sometimes it isn't enough to go through these exercises once. It may be necessary to take these steps frequently until the relief comes. Which brings me to an important point. Some issues are rooted in early childhood and reoccur multiple times in a person's life. On the fifteenth instance, a person's feelings can be overwhelming because they are not just grappling with a current event, but the feelings associated with each of fifteen occurrences. An emotional overreaction occurs when feelings that correlate with multiple events surface all at once. (It's the double boiler effect.)

Finally, pray and ask Jesus to take the feelings. Tell Him you are giving them to Him. Watch to see what happens on the screen in your mind. I once asked Jesus to take my shame, then on the screen in my mind, I saw Him coming with a bulldozer to take it all away. I had to laugh out loud. You may be surprised, He's so creative!

I love how Mark Virkler describes inner healing, "allowing God to replace the pictures in the art gallery of your mind; removing pictures that do not have Jesus in them and replacing them with pictures that do have Jesus in them." Wouldn't a full gallery of Jesus pictures make for a sound heart and mind?

EMOTIONAL WALLS

Just like Pharaoh ordered the children of Israel to make bricks, the enemy is always looking for ways to make bricks in our lives too. Each brick can represent an event, and before we know it, a brick wall can develop inside, separating us from God and others. What cements the bricks together? Inner vows, resentments, and unforgiveness form a paste that hardens like a rock.

Rejection is a good example for wall building. A sense of rejection can enter in the womb if a baby is unwanted. At birth, if the baby doesn't bond with mother, fears of abandonment and rejection increase and another set of bricks are laid as a foundation. Then if an older sibling is mean to the child and mother doesn't come to the rescue, the walls of rejection begin to climb. Every act of abuse and neglect in a child's life is an extreme form of rejection. At school, if the child is teased or ridiculed, that's one more brick each time it happens. By puberty, unrequited affections become stumbling stones as well. Then into adulthood, getting rejected for a job or turned down at the school of your dreams, can feel deeply personal. Each rejection includes a packet of other feelings; sorrow, pain, anger, bitterness. Over a lifetime, rejection can create brick walls that seem insurmountable. Then when life deals another hard blow, a job loss, death, betrayal or infidelity, all those pent-up feelings of rejection can implode at once.

At those difficult times, we can carefully go through the rubble, and hand each event, each brick to Jesus. And let Him mend our broken heart. It is often necessary to examine what we believed about ourselves with each wounding and look for any inner vows. Usually, the enemy has interjected a lie that made the pain worse. Working with Jesus or a trusted minister, those beliefs can be exposed by the light and truth can be incorporated into the healing. The stronghold will topple; then it is easy to evacuate the enemy with a simple command to go.

ENEMY STRONGHOLD OR REPRESSED EMOTIONS

It's not uncommon for people in deliverance ministry to presume most problems are demonic in origin. But I'd like to share a story with you that illustrates the fact that pent-up emotions are often the culprit and it is wise to address emotional care first.

One of my dearest friends Sharon, also a deliverance minister, said to me one day "Kay, I think I'm harboring an offense. I keep repenting for it, but it doesn't go away."

I asked her to share what was bothering her. About six months prior she underwent extensive reconstructive surgery on her right foot. The doctor reassured her the surgery would resolve the pain she was having and she would be able to walk again like normal. Sharon's insurance company preauthorized payment for the surgery, and it proceeded as planned. Recovery from the surgery was very painful and six months later, she still couldn't walk very well or walk any distance.

"After they fused the joints and put in the plates and screws, my foot doesn't bend. I don't have a foot, I have a flipper!" she exclaimed.

After the surgery, the insurance company refused to pay for the procedure and she was left in pain, unable to walk, with a mountain of medical bills to pay.

"I keep forgiving the doctor, but it's still a problem in my heart," she said sadly.

"Sharon," I answered gently, "that's not a spirit of offense, that's a feeling. It sounds like you're angry."

"I am angry!" Sharon said. "He told me I would be able to walk again. But I can't! My foot doesn't bend so I can't go upstairs very well. I can't exercise and I've put on weight since the surgery. On top of all of that, I now owe thousands of dollars in medical bills!"

I just listened as she poured out her heart. She hadn't allowed herself to feel the anger that was building deep inside. As she released the pent-up feelings, she gave voice to her anger. Then her tears began to flow.

"I don't know if I will ever be able to walk right again. When the prayer team was downtown today, I felt left out because I had to stay behind and you girls went off without me." Now sobbing, the grief swelled and she said, "I feel so sad!"

I replied, "Sharon, this isn't because you haven't forgiven or you are harboring an offense. You've done that work. These are powerful feelings that deserve to be heard. Your feelings are important. I'm so glad you shared them with me."

Sharon's circumstances didn't change, but her heart did. God has used these trials in her life to bless those she touches in ministry today. He really does work all things together for our good (Romans 8:28).

The key to effectively managing difficult emotions is addressing the feeling with the LORD. Take a break from the circumstance and spend some time in His presence. When angry, take a long walk or soak in the bathtub and discuss your anger with Him until it is resolved. Give Him the big feelings, and let Him speak into your heart. But do it today.

Some of my deepest healing moments with the LORD happened when I imagined Him holding me and I had a good cry on His shoulder.

Emotions are not the enemy. Emotions were designed by God. Feelings are a part of life. Just like everything else, we need to submit them to His Lordship and allow Him to work in and through them as we go from glory to glory in Him.

WHAT I LEARNED FROM EATING DISORDERS

For most of my life, I struggled with eating disorders. It began before the age of five, with a love for sweets. Then it morphed from compulsive overeating to anorexia and bulimia in my early adolescence. By adulthood, food was more than a comfort, it was an obsession. I spent years in therapy trying to figure it out, and then five years with deliverance ministers. What I discovered was that it wasn't a cognitive behavioral issue, or an issue of demonic spirits, although both were components. It wasn't really about what I was eating; it was a matter of what was eating me. It was an emotional issue.

Repressed or suppressed emotions are a breeding ground for addictive behaviors. In the left brain, I cognitively knew how to eat properly. But the right brain, where the emotions and trauma memories are stored, would override my left brain every time. This quote from Joyce Meyer in "The Everyday Life Bible" sums this up well. "Emotions tempt us to take the easy way, to do what feels good for the moment. Wisdom moves us to take the way that seems hard at first, but later on we find that it leads to life."

I ate and obsessed about my weight to avoid my feelings and deeply buried trauma memories. Food was a method of avoidance for me. I could fuss about the fat grams and calories and ignore the anger I felt toward my mother. It wasn't until I got abstinent with food, that I began to feel and recover emotionally. Grappling with those horrific feelings was a very challenging experience, but it drew me closer to Jesus and from that journey I developed many of the concepts contained herein.

HEALTHY EMOTIONAL LIVING

What does healthy emotional living look like? I suppose it is an ideal rather than the norm for most people. It's a journey day to day wherein we seek to be our most authentic self and not sacrifice who we are to co-dependent behaviors and attitudes. To be healthy emotionally we experience our feelings and don't try repressing or denying them. We don't allow others to tell us how we "should" feel. Rather we know how we really feel. This doesn't mean we express or emote our feelings indiscriminately. Instead, we choose wisely who to share our feelings with and when the timing is appropriate.

Stephen Covey in his best seller "7 Habits of Highly Effective People" stated that between stimulus and response is the point of choice.

Stimulus – Choice – Response

With food addiction, the process went like this:

Feeling – Avoidance – Food

This could be true for any addiction problem:

Pain – Avoidance – Substance/behavior

A healthy emotional response looks like this:

Pain – Acknowledgment – Processing

As ministers and followers of Christ we can set a healthy emotional example by working through our own feelings and encouraging others to do the same.

CHAPTER 10

GRAPPLING WITH GRIEF

Time Magazine's cover story, April 24th, 2017 issue was titled, "Let's Talk About Grief; An unlikely new mission for Sheryl Sandberg." Sheryl lost her husband unexpectedly at age 47 and then lost her emotional bearing. As the mother of two young children, and the COO of Facebook, she was no stranger to life's challenges. But grief radically transformed her life.

Journalist Belinda Luscombe wrote in the above article;

> Dying is not a technical glitch of the human operating system, it's a feature. It's the only prediction we can make at birth that we can bank on. Everyone will die, and it's very likely somebody we love will die before we do. And yet the bereaved are often treated like those to whom something unnatural or disgraceful has happened. People avoid them, don't invite them out, fall silent when they enter the room. The grieving are often isolated when they most need community.

The article went on to explain, when someone is grieving, it is hard to know what to say. If you ask a question you may wonder, "Will it reopen a gaping wound?" Talking about the weather may be polite, but not very helpful. Simple questions like "How are you?" may seem overwhelming to someone grappling with grief, but asking, "How are you today?" may seem more manageable. Simple "I" statements that clearly communicate your care and concern such as, "I'm here for you," and "I love you," may pave the way to precious healing moments for someone grieving.

In her groundbreaking book "On Death & Dying" in 1969, Elizabeth Kubler-Ross outlined the five stages of grief that many are familiar with today. These stages are denial, anger, bargaining, depression, and acceptance. But did you know, people may go through these stages every time they lose a job, a marriage or a home? Even when children leave the nest, we may need to grieve. For people in trauma recovery, they may go through these stages with each trauma memory that is revealed, and again, when they realize the enormity of the cumulative losses in their life. At least that was true for me. As I reflect on the years behind me, grief played a major role in each scene of my life's journey. It was as though I couldn't get from point A to point B without first grappling with my losses.

When our youngest son left the nest, my husband and I thought we would welcome the next chapter of our lives. Instead, we both sank into a lengthy depression. I was in denial at first, thinking it was no big deal. Then my attentions turned to the failures in my childrearing, my marriage, and my life, and I became angry with myself and my husband. But there was nothing I could do to fix the past, and there was no amount of bargaining that would resolve the pain. I felt sucked into a dark vacuum of sadness and depression. For me, it was so debilitating that I insisted we sell the house and move because I couldn't face the empty bedrooms. Rather than embrace this major life change, I fought with it like a seasoned warrior and it lingered on for years. When I was finally able to accept the empty nest, it was because I had finally grappled with the emptiness inside of me, and invited Jesus to transform me through it.

Grief, although just five little letters, stretches over a myriad of emotions like an umbrella. It seems grief takes on a life of its own, demanding, unrelenting and powerful, until it has reshaped and redefined our lives.

EXTERNALIZING GRIEF

I had the privilege of ministering to an older woman who was grieving over her marriage. She and her husband had been married for what seemed like a lifetime. Looking back over those years broke her heart. She came to me looking for answers that I didn't have. Sometimes she was angry, other times sad and remorseful. There wasn't much I could say that would help. Every morning she woke up to the man she married and wished her life had been different. Every week she would come to see me, and all I could do was listen. Finally, she signed up for a grief class at church, which changed her life. Her assignment for the class was to create something that she could share to represent her grief.

She went to Goodwill and bought herself a big straw hat. Next, she purchased black netting at the fabric store to cover her from head to foot. She carefully wrote out each loss she experienced in her marriage and found objects to symbolize each one. When she gave her presentation to her grief class, she released each symbol and finally, the black netting. With this simple act, she externalized her feelings and gave them a voice. Underneath the netting was the straw hat with words on it that represented how she wanted to face her future. And with that, she stepped out of her grief and into a new chapter in her life. Sometimes it takes more than just grappling with feelings; it may take a physical action to shift us from one place to the next.

Twenty years ago, I was recovering trauma memories involving the loss of babies from three separate pregnancies. (In later years, I remembered the loss of three more babies.) The grief was all consuming. I cried all the time, sometimes uncontrollably and unexpectedly. Most days it was all I could do to get out of bed in the morning and go to work. Had it not been for the children I had to come home to in the evening, I don't know that I would have survived the pain. My therapist suggested I hold a memorial for my babies, as a way of finding closure. As I considered ways to memorialize them, I looked for a symbol to represent their life; something that would outlast me. I thought of an evergreen tree. I purchased three beautiful young saplings from the nursery and drove out to a forested area, not far from our home. Somehow, digging into the soft earth and crying over the hole in my heart brought healing. My tears watered, my hands planted, and life came from death.

Jesus, speaking of His own impending death said, *"Truly, truly, I say to you, unless a grain of wheat falls into the earth and dies, it remains alone; but if it dies, it bears much fruit"* (John 12:24, New American Standard Bible).

We can't run from grief, it will find us. Grieving is part of living fully. But we can learn how to be authentic with ourselves and minister Christ's love to others in the middle of life's toughest storms. Jesus also gave us a promise to hold onto when we grieve. *"Blessed are those who mourn for they shall be comforted"* (Matthew 5:4).

CHAPTER 11

FEAR, ANXIETY AND WORRY

Fear, anxiety, and worry seem to run together. The big three cluster together with stress and cause untold harm to our physical and emotional well-being. Most people will readily admit these emotions can be toxic but don't know how to maneuver through them.

Is it a sin to worry or feel fear? Jesus told us *"Fear not"* in Matthew 10:26, 10:28 and 10:31. And He commanded us not to worry four times in the book of Matthew (Matthew 6:25, 6:31, 6:34 and 10:19). Although God wired us with emotions such as fear for our survival, He doesn't want us to be stuck in these emotions. Over time they create problems for us spiritually, emotionally and physically. Instead, our Creator wants us to trust in Him and work through difficult emotions. Rather than focusing on the aspect of sin, I am suggesting we focus on the root cause of habitual issues with fear, stress, anxiety and worry, so we can walk in freedom and good health.

Most of my life, I grappled with these emotions habitually. It seemed I couldn't go a day without worrying about something such as finances, my children, relationships or work. I was constantly obsessing over one thing or another, and it took its toll on my health. Some years ago, I went to the doctor for my annual check-up and the doctor found a lump.

"A lump?" I questioned.

"Well, we won't know what it is until we run some tests" she replied. My stress meter went from 0 to 100 immediately. I choked back the tears and left the doctor's office nearly hysterical. The moment

I got in the car, I called my friend Sarah.

"The doctor found a lump!" I cried.

Calmly Sarah replied, "Good, maybe now you will finally deal with that root of fear you have been nursing for years."

That was not what I wanted to hear, but I knew she was right. She told me she would send me a prayer based upon the teachings of Henry W. Wright that I could use to stand against the fear. She said, "I don't care if you have to say this prayer fifty times a day, you are going to get victory over fear."

The essence of the prayer went something like this:

1. Heavenly Father, I renounce and reject the spirits of fear, stress, anxiety and worry. Please forgive me for all my participation with these spirits and wash me clean.
2. I surrender my heart to you and I cast all my care, all my anxieties, all my worries, all my concerns, once and for all, on you because you care for me affectionately and watchfully. (Based upon 1 Peter 5:7 Amplified Version.)
3. Spirits of fear, stress, anxiety, and worry, I command you off my hypothalamus gland, my adrenal glands, and every cell and tissue of my body, in the Name of Jesus Christ. I command you to leave my mind, body, soul, and spirit, and go immediately to the feet of Jesus Christ, in the power of His shed blood and in His authority. Holy Spirit I ask you to drive them out with the fire of heaven.
4. Body, I direct you to release all fear, anxiety, and stress. All adrenaline and cortisol levels are directed down to normal levels. Body, receive the peace of God into every nerve, organ, and cell in the Name of Jesus Christ. (It is a good idea to exhale the stress and fear, then slowly breathe in the peace of God.)

5. Mind and emotions receive your healing. Receive the peace of God that transcends all understanding. (Imagine warm anointing oil flowing over you.)

6. I declare, "God has not given me a spirit of fear, but of power, and of love and of a sound mind" (2 Timothy 1:7). I receive the peace of God which transcends all understanding and guards my heart and mind in Christ Jesus. (Paraphrased - Philippians 4:7)

7. Holy Spirit please fill me with your grace, peace, and healing virtue. Please show me anytime these spirits attempt to steal the peace you've given me. Thank you, LORD, for my victory!

Admittedly, I had to say the prayer several times a day. I went for ultrasounds and tests that measured the lump and provided the doctor with lots of data. Then I was scheduled to see a specialist but the soonest she could get me in was six weeks. "What?" I thought, "I can't wait that long! I'm freaking out! What if it's cancer?"

ROOT CAUSES

I kept praying and seeking the LORD. As the weeks folded one into the next, I continued to pray against fear, anxiety, and worry. Finally, one day the Holy Spirit whispered, "You're frightened and worried because you don't trust Me."

Of course, He was right, but I didn't want to admit it. Why wasn't I trusting God in this? I deeply searched my soul. God had always been faithful to me. But this was different. Or was it? Over, and over again, the LORD whispered reassurances to my heart, but it wasn't changing how I felt. For some reason, I couldn't believe and receive what He was saying.

I wasn't afraid of dying. This was an even deeper issue. Then I realized I didn't trust God to protect me from physical pain. My heart cried out, "God, you didn't protect me from the pain of childhood abuse, how do I know I can trust you to protect me from more pain?" There it was, the ugly truth.

Until I could get honest with myself and face the core issue at the root of the fear directly, I couldn't receive from Him. And I couldn't stay free of the fear, regardless of the number of times I stood against it in prayer.

TRUSTING GOD

Full of tender mercy He seemed to say, "I was there for you then, I'm here for you now. No matter what you walk through, I will be there with you and I will see you through. Will you trust me?"

The moment required a full surrender to the LORD. No matter what lay ahead I was determined to trust Him. It was a conscious decision of my will.

I remembered what my pastor once said about his health, after he had battled Leukemia for 23 years, he said, "My body belongs to the LORD. This is His problem, not mine."

I declared out loud, "My body belongs to You, God. I trust You to see me through any pain I must endure. I trust You to heal me or take me home to be with You."

Later, the Holy Spirit reminded me of something I used to do as a child in the family swimming pool. I used to float on my back to relax in the water. With exercise induced asthma, if I over exerted, I could have an asthma attack. I discovered, the more I panicked, the tighter my lungs would get. But if I could relax and float on my back, the attack would subside. Holy Spirit impressed upon me the need to trust Him like I was floating on my back. Closing my eyes, I could imagine the water holding my head above the water. When I relaxed and trusted, I could float effortlessly and I could breathe. The fear soon subsided. I gave all my worries and concerns to Him, certain that no matter what happened, God had me in the palm of His hand. By the time I got in to see the specialist, the lump was gone! Faith triumphed over fear.

EXTENDED TESTING

Some years later, I faced another extended test related to fear, anxiety, and worry. My circumstances were desperate. My husband and I had separated after 19 years together and I was living alone in a third-floor apartment. I lost my job at the church and simultaneously felt I had lost my church family. Unemployed, lonely, and severely depressed, my faith took a beating. Everything that could go wrong did. My mother died, I had to stop doing ministry, and my relationship with my daughter was terribly strained. Then my health took a nosedive and I started living with constant abdominal pain. It was so severe at times that I was completely debilitated. After a battery of tests, the doctor concluded my problem was irritable bowel syndrome. That's when I discovered the digestive tract is like a second brain. When the emotions of fear, stress, and anxiety would arise, so did the tummy troubles.

My friend Sarah was so concerned for me that she said decidedly, "You're coming with me to Redmond."

"What's in Redmond?" I replied.

"An old-fashioned revival meeting in a big red barn!" she said. I didn't want to go, but Sarah insisted. It probably saved my life.

With hundreds of people in attendance, an itinerant minister called me out of the crowd and ministered to me as though I was the only one there. She prayed over me for a moment and then she said, "Honey, do you remember the song "Jesus Loves Me?"

I just stood there sobbing and nodded "yes" as snot ran down my face.

Then she began to sing over me, "Yes, Jesus loves me, yes, Jesus loves me, yes Jesus loves me, the Bible tells me so." As she sang, the grief that had welled in my soul burst out in wailing sobs. Her song of love and deliverance set me free from depression.

"Now your prescription" she continued with a great big smile, "is to sing that song three times a day until you are completely well again."

Such a simple song, such a simple message, reached the very depths of my soul. I don't know when my heart had stopped believing Jesus loved me. It was unspoken, it happened gradually, one heartache after another, until the lie somehow took root. Without Jesus my life was unbearable, frightening, and worrisome.

Believing God was good and He loved me was the cornerstone of my faith. Every day I sang that simple song. My faith began to rise and my fears and anxieties began to dissipate. Then I took a big empty coffee can and wrote the words "God Can" on it. I made a list of every miracle I needed. There were 17 items on that list. I put them in the God can, and surrendered them to Him. Every time I was tempted to fret, I reminded myself, "God can!"

David said it so well in Psalm 62:1, *"Truly my soul silently waits for God; From Him comes my salvation."*

God's love for me was not dependent on my circumstances, but instead on covenant relationship. The LORD led me to Hosea 2:19-20, *"And I will betroth you to Me forever; yes, I will betroth you to Me in righteousness and justice, in steadfast love, and in mercy. I will even betroth you to Me in stability and in faithfulness, and you shall know (recognize, be acquainted with, appreciate, give heed to, and cherish) the LORD"* (AMP).

My heart pressed into this scripture. I wanted to experience Jesus as my husband (Hosea 2:16). So, I went to Him for everything I needed, from a shoulder to cry on, to gas money for work. He seemed to delight in this new level of dependency upon Him and He showered me with blessings.

My health improved, finances released, and before I knew it I was nearly finished writing my first book. God gave me a fresh vision for a whole new ministry. I had hope again. After several months of continual restoration, the LORD told me to call my husband and ask for a reconciliation. By Thanksgiving, I returned home. The irritable bowel symptoms disappeared and relationships with my family healed. The move home came with just one condition from my husband; he didn't want me to do ministry from home. With that, I founded Restoration Gateway Ministries and opened the doors to a new office space. In all, the LORD had restored all 17 areas of my life.

"In the multitude of my [anxious] thoughts within me, Your comforts cheer and delight my soul." Psalm 94:19 (AMP)

INTERMITTENT BATTLES

Most of the time, people don't experience such extreme circumstances. You may ask, "What about those intermittent times when I suddenly find myself anxious, worried or afraid?"

During those times, the prayer noted earlier in this chapter can be very helpful. Doing a right brain exercise to picture giving Jesus the feelings will help as described in chapter 9, Safely Processing Emotions. And you might also ask the Holy Spirit to help you determine the belief underneath the feelings. Such as, "I'm worried because I believe _____ (Fill in the blank)."

Look for the original wounding that supported that root belief. Often, it's a childhood event interpreted with child-like thinking. Bring it to the LORD for a touch from Him. If you determine the belief revealed doesn't align with scripture renounce it. And speak the truth out loud using scripture, because faith comes by hearing and hearing by the Word of God (Romans 10:17).

Paul Hegstrom, author of "Broken Children, Grown-up Pain" notes that the human mind trusts the sound of our own voice. What we say to ourselves has a tremendous impact. Directly speaking to your emotions to calm down can be quite helpful. Watch that your self-talk isn't negative. What we say is a left-brain activity.

What we picture is a right-brain activity. If you picture something terrible happening, your emotions will rally around that terrible thing and fear will escalate. But if you ask the LORD to provide His picture of the situation, your emotions will calm right down. Because pictures are the language of emotions, what you picture will have a direct impact on how you feel. For example, if my husband is running late coming home from work and I can't reach him by phone, I might picture a car accident and panic. Or, I can ask the LORD for His perspective. I may get an impression the cell phone battery is dead and there is a lot of traffic. Pictures have a direct impact on emotions.

ALIGNMENT PRAYER

One of the prayer tools I also found very effective is an alignment prayer. I first discovered this prayer years ago when taking Timothy Davis' Cleansing Streams class at a local church. The concept is when our triune being: body, soul, and spirit, is properly aligned with the Holy Spirit we can walk in the fruit of the Spirit, namely self-control (Galatians 5:22).

"In the Name of Jesus Christ, I command my body to line-up with my soul. Soul and emotions, line-up with my spirit. And spirit, I command you to line-up with the Holy Spirit and the Word of God. Amen."

Grappling with fear, anxiety, and worry can be challenging. But there is no limit to the creative ideas God will provide to help us overcome and walk in emotional health.

"Why are you cast down, O my soul? And why are you disquieted with me? Hope in God; for I shall yet praise Him, the help of my countenance and my God."

Psalm 42:11

CHAPTER 12

A NEW WINESKIN FOR DELIVERANCE

Spiritual warfare and the ministry of deliverance are subjects that evoke powerful reactions in the Body of Christ. To some, it seems strange and is often misunderstood. Many prefer to avoid the topic altogether, and claim Christians can't have demons. While still others have honed their skills in spiritual warfare to a fine art.

Though nearly one-third of Jesus ministry consisted of deliverance, the Bible provides a modest explanation for this broad topic. Could it be the Holy Spirit intended for us to be dependent on Him directly for the revelation? He probably knew if we had a set of rules we would become legalistic. And maybe in His wisdom, He knew if methods were too detailed, we would become more focused on the methodology than the Deliverer Himself.

Jesus gave us the great commission in Mark chapter 16. In verses 17 and 18 Jesus said, *"And these signs will follow those who believe: In My name they will cast out demons; they will speak with new tongues; they will take up serpents; and if they drink anything deadly, it will by no means hurt them; they will lay hands on the sick and they will recover."* It could be said, casting out demons and ministering healing is part of our calling in Christ.

Holy Spirit has increased revelation to the Church concerning spiritual gifts in recent decades. In the same way, I believe He also wants to increase revelation for deliverance. Since most of this manuscript focuses on emotional care, let's start with the topic of emotion-based spirits.

EMOTION-BASED SPIRITS

There is a difference between emotions and evil spirits. As previously discussed, God wired us with the ability to experience a wide range of emotions. Expressing an emotion does not indicate a person has an evil spirit. However, emotion-based spirits can attach to the soul if emotions are repressed, suppressed, or otherwise mishandled. It's not easy to separate the two when that happens, causing confusion between emotions and emotion-based spirits.

The Church and the Greek mindset have vilified emotions for centuries. As a result, people lack a proper understanding of their emotions and the tools to effectively manage them. I have yet to meet a baby boomer whose parents gave them these skills. Rather than process feelings, people often suppress them, causing an internal environment that will attract demonic spirits. Furthermore, if a person gets stuck in an emotion, infestation can occur as well.

I recall the story of a widow still grieving over the death of her husband many years after his passing. Her adult children were alarmed that she was still crying every day and sought ministerial assistance. The minister asked the woman to break agreement with the spirit of grief, and he cast it out without much fanfare. The crying stopped immediately.

If a person harbors resentment or bitterness in their heart, they will likely have spirits of resentment and bitterness to cast out. The longer unprocessed emotions linger in the heart, the more powerful the associated demonic can become.

Fear is similar. If a person resolves feelings of fear quickly, a stronghold of fear and fear-based spirits won't be an issue. But most people try to hide their fears and anxieties allowing them to fester inside. For trauma survivors with dissociation, fears are often repressed due to the inability to process their feelings at the point of victimization. This requires the minister to lovingly validate feelings, while also assisting in the emotional processing and providing deliverance from infestation without causing additional trauma.

What about anger? How do you know if you have a spirit of anger when you get angry? Tell-tale signs are whether the anger is manageable or not and whether a person can let go of the anger once it is expressed appropriately. One of the challenges with anger is that it can build and become rage or even murderous rage if unresolved. This then requires both emotional care and deliverance. Paul instructed, *"Be angry, and do not sin; do not let the sun go down on your wrath, nor give place to the devil"* (Ephesians 4:26-27).

Emotion-based spirits are relatively easy to evacuate.

1. Emotions need to be processed (felt) and given to Jesus
2. Forgiveness must occur – no forgiveness, no deliverance!
3. Ask the Holy Spirit to expose any lies of the enemy and renounce them
4. Agreements must be broken with the spirits and repentance declared for participation with them
5. A simple command will cast out the spirits

If a person has a history of emotional wounds, the enemy may repeatedly attack a person emotionally. This is evident when emotions go catawampus for no apparent reason. It helps to bring the emotions into alignment with the Holy Spirit as described in the previous chapter and to refute the attack in Jesus mighty name.

"Keep your heart with all diligence, for out of it spring the issues of life" (Proverbs 4:23).

SEVERE DEMONIZATION

Back in the late 1990's when I first learned about deliverance I was afraid to seek help because what I saw on TV terrified me. My only frame of reference was the movie "The Exorcist" and what I saw of a popular minister on television. This minister performed deliverance procedures on SRA survivors on screen by flaunting his authority, engaging in direct confrontation, and screaming at the demons. There was always a sensational fight with spitting, hissing, and people writhing on the floor. The show catapulted the minister to fame at the expense of highly traumatized and dissociated survivors. Looking back, I believe this was a disservice to the Body of Christ by making something intended to bring liberty, a sensational and scary spectacle.

Although put off by what I saw on television, I was desperate for help. A co-worker recommended a minister located just over the Interstate Bridge. I took the afternoon off work and drove to a humble home in Vancouver, Washington. When I arrived, my stomach was churning and I was terribly nauseous. The minister's wife answered the door to a nearly green Christian. She welcomed me inside. This lovely Christian couple spent two hours trying to get demons out of me. They placed a bible on my head and allowed the devils to manifest while I writhed on the floor and they screamed commands for them to leave. A full menagerie of demons tossed me around like a rag doll in a dog's mouth that day. In the end, we were all exhausted and I was no better off than when I arrived.

Knowing what I do now, if demons have legal rights they won't let go. If the minister had me renounce the spiritual legal ground associated with the Satanic and Luciferian rituals I had been subjected to, those demons would have evacuated without such a fight. The reason I share this experience, is to encourage you that there is a better way to get people free. Deliverance doesn't have to be a scary or traumatic experience.

When the LORD brought me to George in 2004, he combined biblical counsel, inner healing, deliverance, and integration methods into each session through his prophetic gifting and the guidance of the Holy Spirit. What had taken nineteen years in therapy, took three hours in a ministry session with George. Holy Spirit directed him like a laser to exactly the areas of my broken heart that needed to be addressed. He never queried the devils for information, he simply asked Holy Spirit. When George commanded devils out they went without a fight because they were forbidden to manifest. It was the most peaceful and effective process I could imagine. The only time I had a physical manifestation, a bit of coughing, occurred as spirits of Freemasonry were evicted. Other than that, it was a very calm process. George, empowered by the Holy Spirit, was the only person that made a tangible difference in my freedom and healing. After just a few months working with George, Holy Spirit released me into ministry with the same anointing.

NEW WINESKIN CONCEPTS

We don't have to allow demons to manifest. And for goodness sake don't hold conversations with devils, they lie! in Mark 1:25 Jesus told demons to be quiet and come out. Any necessary information should be coming from the person receiving ministry and the Holy Spirit. Granted, Jesus did ask "What is your name?" in Mark 5:9. But that was for the readers' benefit. Jesus knew exactly what He was dealing with then and He still does today. It's not about us, how much we know, how much authority we have, it's about Him.

It is not necessary to know the name of every devil being evicted. It's just necessary to know the Name above all names, Jesus. It is sufficient to say, "I command every demon that entered Sally with this event to go now." Similarly, you can cast a big net by saying, "every demon with an assignment to ___ (fill in the blank: cause fear, harm, distress etc.) must evacuate now, and take every demon that entered in with you out as well."

When ministering deliverance for broken parts of the heart (Dissociative Identity Disorder) you can bind every spirit on the alter identities and command them out without combing through names. More information on this topic will be provided in the following chapter.

In the authority of Jesus Christ, we can bind demons to silence and forbid them from manifesting, speaking or operating. "But" you may object, "how do we know when it leaves if it doesn't manifest?" The person will visibly relax and feel lighter. If that's insufficient evidence, you can always ask the Holy Spirit to show you what still needs to go. I'm assuming if you are in ministry, you can hear the Holy Spirit direct you. If you can't, that needs to be resolved first.

I realize what I am suggesting disagrees with a lot of current ministry methods, but if it's possible to get the most radically demon possessed/oppressed individuals on the planet free, such as satanic ritual abuse (SRA) survivors, don't you think these ideas will work with less severe cases? SRA survivors can carry a demonic load involving hundreds of thousands of demons. We can either wrestle to command each devil out or we can break the legal ground, such as specific occult ceremonies that gave it a right to enter in the first place, then they must leave. Calling each one out by name and fighting with them doesn't make sense when there are more effective methods available today.

If a minister is having difficulty identifying the legal ground and getting someone free, another option is to petition the courts of heaven. This method takes deliverance from the battle ground to the court room where hundreds of matters can be addressed at once.

Psalm 82:1 provides a picture of these courts, "God stands in the congregation of the mighty; He judges among the gods." In verses 3 and 4 the Psalmist writes, *"Defend the poor and fatherless; do justice to the afflicted and needy. Deliver the poor and needy; free them from the hand of the wicked."*

Asking God to convene a heavenly court can't be taken lightly or flippantly. But you can prayerfully and respectfully ask the Heavenly Father to hear your case. If you feel the unction of the Holy Spirit to move forward, then prepare the matters to be addressed in advance. With prayer and fasting, a ruling from the highest court in the universe can produce tremendous results. Robert Henderson has an excellent resource available on this topic titled, "Operating in the Courts of Heaven" available on Amazon.com. I believe this is a portion of the new wineskin for freedom today.

For the Church to move in the freedom necessary to advance the Kingdom of God in this hour, I believe, we need to put our experience on the altar and move as the Holy Spirit is leading today. He may show you an even more excellent way (1 Cor. 12:31).

I love the picture of deliverance for the leper in Mark 1:40 and 41. The leper kneels before Jesus and he says, *"If you are willing, you can make me clean."* The next verse says, *"Then Jesus, moved with compassion, stretched out His hand and touched him, and said to him, "I am willing; be cleansed."* No matter the degree of our filth, Jesus is always willing to reach out and cleanse us.

If you are looking for a good opening and closing prayer for deliverance ministry you can download the Ministry Set-up Prayer and the Spiritual Legal Ground List from Restoration Gateway

Ministries "Free Resources," located under the Training tab at www.rgmconnect.com.

"The Spirit of the Lord God is upon Me, because the Lord has anointed Me to preach good tidings to the poor; He has sent Me to heal the brokenhearted, to proclaim liberty to the captives, and the opening of the prison to those who are bound."

Isaiah 61:1

CHAPTER 13

TRAUMA, PTSD, DISSOCIATION & DID

Trauma, PTSD, Dissociation, and Dissociative Identity Disorder are all related conditions. Ministers need to familiarize themselves with these topics and get as much training and education as necessary to properly serve those struggling with these issues. Few people escape childhood without trauma related problems. It's unfortunately quite common to have one or more of these conditions operating in most ministry recipients. Minister's without proper skills or understanding of trauma related disorders can cause harm in their ignorance. If a client is not healing or has become suicidal in your care, refer them to a specialist in ministry or a trusted medical professional.

TRAUMA

"Trauma by definition, is unbearable and intolerable," wrote Dr. Bessel Van Der Kolk, MD in his renowned book, "The Body Keeps the Score." As such, all judgments and legalism aside, we must understand how to love and minister like Jesus when addressing this level of brokenness.

Trauma and dissociation are very broad and complex topics that could span hundreds of pages. For our purposes, in understanding the new wineskin, I will simply attempt to provide a basic understanding in layman's terms so ministers can be acquainted with the subject and in turn provide spiritual and emotional safety for those they encounter in ministry with Dissociative Identity Disorder (DID) and/or Post-Traumatic Stress Disorder (PTSD).

Trauma activates the right brain and deactivates the left. In other words, it is difficult to make logical decisions when a person is in a highly emotional state. Condemning the emotions as the problem simply serves to cause more damage. But isn't that what we do when we tell people, "Can't you just put the past behind you and move on?"

Unprocessed trauma is stored in the right brain. This is one reason, talk therapy doesn't work to resolve trauma. Talking is a left brain analytical exercise. If someone is fearful and you tell them five logical reasons not to feel fear, it won't help. Logic is not the language of the heart, pictures are. I can give you 31 reasons not to do something, but if your emotions are hooked into a trauma there is no amount of reason or logic that will convince you otherwise. The right brain will override reason and logic every time. This explains why diets don't work if people eat for emotional reasons.

Mark Virkler of Communion with God Ministries and Christian Leadership University teaches that we can change the pictures in the mind simply by inviting Jesus into them. By working through imagery, trauma can be released and emotions can heal.

RIGHT BRAIN MINISTRY TO TRAUMA

God taught Jeremiah how to use his right brain in Jeremiah 1:11 and 1:13. He asked, "Jeremiah what do you see?" in both verses. Simply by asking, "What do you see?" can help facilitate the process. Although it sounds easy, some people need some practice activating the right brain, especially if they predominately function in the left.

I want to reassure you the ability to see with the mind's eye or vision is a gift from God. Our Creator designed us with two brain hemispheres fully intending that we would use both. Jesus our role model and example said, *"I speak what I have seen with My*

Father..." John 8:38. The only way to see the Father is through the use of right brain imagery.

Some ministers express concern about performing a new age practice when working with right brain imagery. New age practices counterfeit the real things of the Kingdom of God. If they didn't have value, they wouldn't be copied. Just because the enemy has copied something God intended to bring greater intimacy with Him, doesn't mean we throw the practice out. Instead we use it properly. One way to ensure the enemy doesn't infect a holy process, and to ease your mind, just consecrate the eyes of the heart to God.

In the book of Daniel there are three instances when he "looked" using his spiritual vision: Daniel 7:6, 10:5 and 12:5. Probably the best example of right brain vision can be found in the book of Habakkuk, chapter 2:1, *"I will stand my watch and set myself on the rampart, and watch to see what He will say to me, and what I will answer when I am corrected."*

Art work and creative projects also utilize the right brain. The use of drawing, clay, sand tray objects, and collage are all powerful tools for the right brain to express itself. Trauma can be processed using these methods very effectively. The brain simply needs a mechanism for expression.

By using right brain imagery, a minister can facilitate the connection between their client and the LORD Jesus Christ. Teaching them to sense the presence of the LORD in their spirit and to look for Him in their mind's eye they can effectively bring Jesus into each trauma event for His truth and healing. This is the primary methodology used in life changing inner healing practices.

"Research has shown that mental practice – imagination, visualization, deep thought, and reflection – produces the same physical changes in the brain as it would [by] physically carrying out the same imagined processes." says Dr. Carolyn Leaf in "Who Switched Off My Brain?" When Jesus heals a wound for a trauma survivor using right brain imagery, physically, it has the same effect on the brain as though it really happened! That's truly astounding and encouraging!

POST-TRAUMATIC STRESS DISORDER

Many people that experience trauma will develop PTSD if untreated. The National Institute of Mental Health states, "PTSD is a disorder that develops in some people who have experienced a shocking, scary, or dangerous event." They continue by stating,

> It is natural to feel afraid during and after a traumatic situation. Fear triggers many split-second changes in the body to help defend against danger or to avoid it. This "fight-or-flight" response is a typical reaction meant to protect a person from harm. Nearly everyone will experience a range of reactions after trauma, yet most people recover from initial symptoms naturally. Those who continue to experience problems may be diagnosed with PTSD. People who have PTSD may feel stressed or frightened even when they are not in danger.[9]

Post-traumatic Stress Disorder (PTSD) is developed as a reaction to trauma. It is widely accepted socially and is believed to affect 8% of the general population in the United States. PTSD is closely related to dissociative disorders. In fact, 80-100% of people diagnosed with a dissociative disorder also have a secondary

---

9   https://www.nimh.nih.gov/health/topics/post-traumatic-stress-disorder-ptsd/index.shtml 8.15.17

diagnosis of PTSD. Recent research suggests the risk of suicide attempts among people with trauma disorders may be even higher than among people who have major depression. In addition, there is evidence that people with trauma disorders have higher rates of alcoholism, chronic medical illnesses, and abusiveness in succeeding generations.

Although society has come to accept PTSD, we have yet to accept and understand dissociation, which often accompanies PTSD. What many ministers don't realize is that PTSD is an anxiety disorder, but DID is a splitting of the soul. With PTSD, the brain operates in a hypervigilant state as a means of preventing further trauma. It's as though the body's alarm systems are constantly on high alert. People that are hypervigilant have a strong startle reflex and some experience both social anxiety and discomfort with crowds. A symptom of hypervigilance is sometimes demonstrated in little things like where a person may position themselves in a restaurant, so they can see the exits or sit in a corner where they know there is no one behind them.

Stress hormones chronically course through the bloodstream when a person feels hypervigilant and it is difficult to relax or feel safe. This can cause insomnia which may further compound the anxiety and may accompany depression and substance abuse. When people don't sleep, stress compounds from one day to the next, exacerbating existing problems and sometimes creating new ones.

We have all heard stories of veterans that return from the battlefield with PTSD. Likewise, children growing up in abusive, neglectful, and or dysfunctional homes can suffer from PTSD as well. Not all people that have PTSD have dissociation, but almost all people with dissociation have PTSD.

Dissociation usually begins before a child's personality is well formed before six or seven years old. Once the brain has utilized dissociation as a defense mechanism, a person can split well into adulthood whenever there is a life threatening, highly stressful, or traumatic experience. While in utero and at birth, the brain is primarily operating in the right hemisphere where people experience feelings, creativity, and God. As a child begins to mature around four or five, left-brain abilities to reason and plan develop as well. This explains why nursery school and kindergarten are such fun artistic places for children to learn and grow. After first or second grade, most education, becomes very left-brain focused with mathematics, language, and reading. The personality develops and becomes solid around the age of seven, it is not likely a person will fragment from trauma if experienced for the first time after this age. Therefore, if a man escaped childhood reasonably unscathed, he could enter the battlefield and experience the shock and trauma of war without necessarily splitting. Though the sights and sounds of war may replay in his mind, he won't split, unless there was previous splitting before the age of six or seven. Without the benefit of being able to split, in some ways, the trauma experienced on the battlefield may be more debilitating because the mind can't separate it off. But in the same way, a person can give feelings to the LORD, they can also release pictures, audio files, body memory, and traumatic events in the healing process.

If you are looking for good resources for PTSD ministry, check out the tools provided by Dr. Mike Hutchings of Global Awakenings. The website is: goglobal@globalawakening.com. God can, and He will, heal PTSD if we let Him.

WHAT IS DISSOCIATION?

Dissociation is the mind's provision for the unbearable. It is a fascinating study of the mind body connection as the result of trauma. Psychology Today's definition of DID, "Dissociative Identity

Disorder, formerly referred to as multiple personality disorder, is a condition wherein a person's identity is fragmented into two or more distinct personality states."[10]

In the 1994 edition of "The Diagnostic and Statistical Manual of Mental Disorders-IV," by the American Psychiatric Association, the change from the usage of the term Multiple Personality Disorder (MPD), to Dissociative Identity Disorder, occurred to reflect significant changes in the professional understanding of the disorder, based on empirical research. Dissociative disorders are now understood to be the common effects of severe trauma in early childhood; most typically extreme, repeated physical, sexual, spiritual, and/or emotional abuse.

People with DID can have as few as one alternate identity state in addition to the primary self, or they can have thousands of identities (as in the case of ritual abuse). These identities may be referred to by several names: parts, alters or broken pieces of the heart, just to name a few.

Dissociation is a mental process which produces a lack of connection in a person's thoughts, memories, feelings, actions, or sense of identity. Dissociation causes traumatic information to be disconnected from other information in the mind. For example, during a traumatic experience a person may dissociate the memory of the place and circumstances of the trauma from his ongoing memory resulting in a temporary mental escape from the fear and pain of the trauma. In most cases a memory gap surrounding the experience is evident. Because this process can produce changes in memory, people who frequently dissociate often find their sense of personal history and identity are affected.

---

10   https://www.psychologytoday.com/conditions/dissociative-identity-disorder-multiple-personality-disor-der 8.15.17

Dissociative Identity Disorder (DID) is more common than most people realize. Because it is an amazing defense mechanism, it may be well hidden. Twenty years ago, it was reported most people with DID spent an average of seven years in therapy before DID was even identified. I was one of the lucky ones, it only took three years and two different practitioners to recognize it in me. Back in the 1990s, MPD/DID was a new area of exploration for pioneering clinicians and researchers. Today, medical professionals are getting more education on the subject.

Minister's also need training because the brokenhearted will often seek ministry. Don't let the big terms and psychobabble discourage you from learning more. You don't have to be a clinician to minister love and recognize a broken heart. But you need to be prepared to refer your client if at any point you feel in over your head, or if your client is suicidal and not responding well to ministerial care.

In very simple terms, you could say dissociation is a broken heart. Jesus told us in Luke 4:18, that He came to heal the brokenhearted and to proclaim liberty to the captives, fulfilling Isaiah 61:1. In scripture, the word for "soul" is often used synonymously with the word "heart." It is also said that the human heart is about the size of a person's closed hand. If you can picture a closed hand, trauma is like a knife that cuts off a thumb. Imagine the thumb represents a disconnected part of the soul. Dis – separated from association or dissociation. This part can hold trauma memory, emotions, and demonic infestation. This part is generally age arrested at the time of the trauma. The mind, in its wisdom, usually places an amnesic barrier around the part and tucks it away, down deep inside. The more horrific the trauma the more amnesia is present. In a very real sense, that broken part experiences rejection by the rest of the heart, because the psyche has a need to deny what has happened and therefore pushes the part away.

George once told me he asked the LORD where he could find DID in the scripture. The Holy Spirit directed him to Psalm 147:2-4, which reads, *"The LORD builds up Jerusalem; He gathers together the outcasts of Israel. He heals the brokenhearted and binds up their wounds. He counts the number of the stars; He calls them all by name."*

Isn't that a beautiful picture? Jerusalem, in this context, is a metaphor for the soul, and the stars symbolize the fragments of the heart. This is a promise too, that Jesus will gather the broken pieces of the heart and bind up their wounds. The ministry of healing the broken heart is truly a ministry of reconciliation (2 Cor. 5:18). It is about reconciliation to self, God, and others.

To illustrate the value of dissociation, imagine a child who awakens to sexual abuse by her father in the morning and then must perform on a spelling test in the afternoon. If the child goes to school with the recent trauma on her mind, she won't be able to function at school. But if the child immediately dissociates and the psyche fractures off a little piece of her heart, then her conscious awareness of the traumatic event is completely wrapped in amnesia and tucked away. Fracturing is not something a child can control, it is an involuntary response of the brain. In most cases, the fractured part essentially goes to sleep and is only awakened if a similar event or a trigger occurs. The child heading to school will have no conscious memory of the morning's event and will be able to function as though the sexual abuse didn't happen. But the price paid is a separation from self, a blanket of amnesia, and a broken identity.

People with DID can be highly functional, capable of successfully running multimillion-dollar enterprises and juggling family and civic responsibilities as well. It's a matter of successful compartmentalization and effective information processing internally.

DISSOCIATED IDENTITY DISORDER (DID) INDICATORS

Below are a few of the more obvious indicators of DID. In addition to this list are also a few common characteristics, such as very high intelligence, creativity, and unusual spiritual abilities.

- Memory loss
- Handwriting changes
- Rapid voice, mood, and mannerism changes
- Hearing internal voices
- Inordinate indecision, especially with clothing
- Denial of behavior witnessed by others

MEMORY LOSS

One of the telling signs of DID is significant memory loss, especially any block after the age of five. On the Restoration Gateway ministry questionnaire, we specifically ask if people can remember events before the age of ten years old. If they indicate that they can't, we know more investigative work may be necessary to determine the cause. Most people with dissociation struggle with both short-term and long-term memory issues due to amnesia and fracturing.

When I was asked about my childhood by a therapist in the 1990's, I thought I could remember everything just fine. Until my therapist asked me to write down on blank sheets of paper what I remembered for each year of my life. To my dismay, I had very little conscious memory of each year. My mind had constructed a pseudo history from the few fragments of memory I did have and strung them together to bridge any gaps. I could remember where I lived, where I went to school, and in most cases the names of my teachers. Beyond that, I had very little memory, which was quite a shocking revelation for me. This exercise highlighted the denial and memory gaps operating at the time.

HANDWRITING CHANGES

Other symptoms of dissociation include handwriting that changes from printing to cursive or dramatic changes in appearance from one writing to another. This was apparent to me during my adult years in recovery when I noticed the handwritten file folders in my desk drawer. I was ashamed to note the differences in writing styles and immediately had labels typed to hide it.

RAPID VOICE, MOOD, AND MANNERISM CHANGES

When a dissociated identity comes fully forward, it is termed taking executive control of the body. An observer may notice rapid changes in voice tone, mood, and mannerisms. For example, a three-year-old child may come forward with a higher pitched voice than the adult. The child may be frightened, insecure, and looking for mommy. Young child alters have a much smaller vocabulary, but they may be vocal about their needs and concerns. A child will have different facial expressions than an adult, and may do things like thumb sucking or crying. I keep pillows, blankets, and stuffed animals handy for little ones, so they can feel safer when they come forward. Young alters have been essentially frozen in time, so when they appear they may not understand why their hands are so big or why the dog doesn't look the same. It's important if this happens to gently acclimate the child to their new surroundings. Minister to them, but also, make sure the primary presenting identity is co-conscious while the child is forward. Most alters reside in the back of the mind, but when they speak or take executive control of the body, it is apparent they have come forward.

HEARING INTERNAL VOICES

Not all people that hear voices inside are crazy. Often, they are dissociative. What they are hearing is the voices of the various alters inside. These alters come forward especially when under stress. A person may be able to hear the Holy Spirit, various alters, and sometimes they can hear demonic spirits. Even the most rational person can have difficulty discerning between them. To follow is a series of practical steps I found helpful in these instances:

1. Bind the demonic spirits to silence and forbid them from manifesting, operating, or speaking until a deliverance session can be arranged.
2. Respectfully speak to the alters inside and ask them to step back and be quiet for a time so you can clearly hear the voice of the Holy Spirit.
3. Ask the Holy Spirit to increase the volume and help discern His voice.

INORDINATE INDECISION, ESPECIALLY WITH CLOTHING

This isn't the same thing as a teenager trying to find a dress for prom. No, this is more challenging. I almost laugh as I imagine the familiar pile of clothes on the floor. Alters can be different ages in the body. They may have varying taste in clothing congruent with age, function, and individual taste. So, when it comes to choosing clothes, if there are several alters up front, it can be very difficult to decide what to wear. Sexual alters may prefer more risqué choices, Christian alters may feel more modest and some alters associate colors with mind control programming. Is it any wonder getting dressed in the morning is a bit of an ordeal? The good news is that there are ways to manage internal conflict with parts until healing and integration can take place. A very helpful resource for more information is "The Dissociative Identity Disorder Sourcebook" by Deborah Bray Haddock.

DENIAL OF BEHAVIOR WITNESSED BY OTHERS

A hallmark of dissociation is the denial of behavior clearly observed by others. How can this happen? Different parts are holding different time sequences in memory. Let me better explain this by using the illustration of a stage and character actors.

THE DID STAGE

To understand how alters operate, imagine a stage. Out front is the person you normally see. This may be a "host personality" or the main aspect of self. This is the person the world sees. When dissociation occurs the person out front may slip back behind the stage curtain and another character will come out to take center stage. Having center stage is having executive control of the body. When this happens, if the alternate identity is amnesic, the adult self may not remember the event at all. This is called "losing time." Losing time is not a good thing, because anything can happen while the main self is behind the curtain.

After a traumatic incident where I was physically threatened in my work environment, years ago, my main personality slipped back behind the curtain and another part came forward to manage the situation. When I came back, I was behind the wheel of my car, in an unfamiliar part of town. I had no idea where I was or how I got there. Obviously, this is not safe. I don't know what I may have said when I left the office or what behavior my co-workers may have observed. I simply had no memory of that block of time. If they had confronted me on my behavior, I likely would have denied it because I had no memory of it.

Ideally, it is best to have co-consciousness. This means the main self is forward and any other parts that need to talk are on the stage together at the same time. They can hear and see each other enabling them to communicate. Each of them knows what is happening. Co-consciousness is a good safety rule to prevent losing time. This rule can be implemented by simply stating to the system of alters, "The primary or host self must always be present when others want to come forward."

WHY IS THIS INFORMATION SO IMPORTANT FOR MINISTERS?

If a person is dissociative, they won't heal unless the fragmented parts of the heart are addressed. For example, when George was ministering to me on the topic of food addiction he said, "Katie, you're not overeating, you're eating for twenty!" There were twenty separate identities inside that were operating in food addiction. When Jesus brought healing and integration to those parts I experienced real freedom from food addiction for the first time in my adult life.

Failure to work with dissociated parts can also make it more difficult to perform deliverance because different alters may hold legal rights to various demonic entities through an act of their independent will or trauma experience. I have observed many instances where women battle a spirit of Jezebel repeatedly with little or no success. They may think they need a more powerful minister, when in fact, they need to come to terms with an alter inside causing the problem. In multigenerational occult families, it is common to find Jezebelic alters that have been dedicated from infancy to Jezebel. They take on the characteristics of Jezebel, the demonic power, and authority of Jezebel. They take vows and initiation rites to serve Jezebel as they age. If the alter doesn't come to repentance it will be nearly impossible to get the woman free from the spirit. But God!

In ignorance, ministers sometimes say and do harmful things if they don't understand dissociation. Some ministries insist people with DID must repent for dissociating. Why would someone need to repent for something they have no control over? Especially since DID involves early childhood trauma before the age of accountability. Insisting a person repent for the involuntary mechanism of dissociation at the point of trauma, is shaming. It is an act of both spiritual and emotional abuse.

Misinformation is rampant in ministry circles on the topic of DID. I had a licensed clinician, who was also ordained as a pastor tell me, "Once all the demons are gone you will no longer have alters." This is simply not true. Broken pieces of the soul are very different from demonic entities. Although most alters have demonic on them resulting from the wounding, they are two separate things.

Ministries that claim instant healing and deliverance can be a disservice to survivors. There are several ministries that claim they can deliver and integrate large DID systems in one sitting. I don't believe it is possible, unless God sovereignly does a miracle. The reason is *human beings need time to process emotional trauma.* We aren't just talking about deliverance, which requires lots of work for SRA survivors, but processing grief, anger, pain, and internal conflicts, takes time. It doesn't take 25 years anymore. But it does take some time, two or three years on average. I do believe God is accelerating the process, but He can only heal parts willing to be healed. People leave these instant healing sessions believing they are whole, when often they are not. Admitting there are still problems and alters inside, can be hard to face after being told, "you're all fixed." In some cases, people have gone back to these ministries with problems and they are told, "You didn't have enough faith," thereby blaming the survivor. The key is a holistic approach to healing that ministers to the emotions, the parts, physical issues, as well as deliverance. That process takes as long as it takes, it can't be short circuited. Human beings are very complex. Emotional care and emotional healing take time.

Do not attempt to cast out alters or "get rid" of alters. This could also be characterized as emotional and spiritual abuse. Alters are not demons to get rid of. They are parts of a fractured self. Healing is about reconciliation; not rejection. The objective in the healing process is to restore the shattered soul to wholeness.

The caveat, is that if parts refuse repeatedly to turn from evil and they are causing problems with the rest of the system. I have worked with alters of this nature for six months or longer before they finally agreed to receive Jesus. The best method for transformation is to insist they meet Jesus and spend some time in His presence. 99% of the time, when parts really experience Him, they are willing to receive from Him. Only in 1% of my cases has it ever been necessary to ask Jesus to remove an alter personality. He is always reluctant to do it, because the gifts and unique qualities of that part of self are lost forever. It's a last resort option. Instead it is best to persevere, evangelize, and love until the breakthrough comes.

DELIVERANCE PROCEDURES AND DID

People that have experienced significant traumas are more likely to have significant demonic infestation. Trauma creates an open door for the enemy, much like a gaping wound attracts infection. The blood of Jesus is our antiseptic. Once the infection is removed healing begins.

Old-fashioned deliverance methods can cause more harm than good for people with DID. If ministers yell and scream at demons during deliverance this can be terrifying to young child alters and have a detrimental effect on the entire healing process. Parts that might otherwise disclose their pain or activities, will instead hide and refuse to cooperate. Older alters and cult loyal alters may rise-up in defiance if a minister starts barking commands that they find threatening. If it's necessary to be firm to get a devil out, explain what you are doing so the alters understand.

Most trauma inducing events that cause dissociation also cause tremendous fear. As a result, people with DID have many internal parts frozen in time, stuck in their fear. Standard deliverance procedures to renounce and repent for the fear, won't work with DID. There could be an army of alters that are afraid. Telling someone, "just walk in faith and renounce the fear" is not realistic for a system with lots of parts. All of the parts holding fear have to be addressed, in some cases, individually. When survivors are unable to break free of the fear, sometimes, they are shamed by ministers that don't understand. It's not a matter of faith, it's a matter of dissociation. Each little part may hold fear, especially very young ones. Reassuring them that they are safe now and encouraging them to give the fear to Jesus is far more effective. It is possible to ask the Holy Spirit to gather all the frightened alters into the presence of the LORD for healing, but sometimes there are stragglers that hide when called.

When occultism and witchcraft are the sources of childhood trauma and dissociation, as is the case with satanic ritual abuse, significant issues of spiritual legal ground must be addressed to eradicate the demonic. If demonic spirits refuse to leave, yelling won't solve the problem and neither is ganging up on a person. Breaking legal ground is the answer. Once the legal rights have been broken, the enemy must leave. Even upon a whispered command, the demonic will evacuate. A Spiritual Legal Ground List is available for ministers under Free Resources on the rgmconnect.com website.

Other effective resources for SRA deliverance can be found on Amanda Buys' website www.kanaanministries.org or Yvonne Kitchen's website www.fruitfulvine.org.

In the next section, we will discuss how to bring healing to the broken heart.

CHAPTER 14

MINISTRY TO THE BROKEN HEART

Reclaiming the broken pieces of the heart/soul can be painstaking work but it is immensely rewarding. It is so important that ministers are careful to respect and love the dissociated parts they encounter to facilitate the healing process. Even if the parts are snarly, be kind and merciful. It will go a long way in building trust. When you consider the fact that parts have reason not to trust anyone, it's especially important that ministers are trustworthy, loving, and willing to earn their trust, like Jesus with skin on.

Systems can be as simple as one or two parts or highly sophisticated and complex comprising thousands of alters as is the case with satanic ritual abuse. Typically, the healing process for dissociated identities starts slowly and builds momentum as trust is developed and parts see others receive healing. In time, it is possible to bring thousands of parts to Jesus at one sitting for integration. Truly, I don't believe it is possible to fully heal and integrate a highly sophisticated SRA system without the active presence of Jesus. His miracle working power is beyond my explanation.

There are a few more things to know about the fragments of the broken heart. First, did you know that alters can be either male or female regardless of the gender of the human body? Genesis 1:27 declares, *"So God created man in His own image; in the image of God He created him; male and female He created them."*

If a little girl feels she would have been safer as a boy, her psyche may create male alters to meet this need. Or if a little boy perceives his sisters get all the love and attention, he may fracture into little girl alters at the point of trauma. Children that are sexually abused sometimes create alters of the opposite sex to cope with sexual trauma and may struggle with sexual identity as a result. Again, it is important to withhold judgment but instead minister love and mercy.

Next, depending on the severity of a trauma, splitting can occur based upon the five senses. One part may hold the visual images, another the audio file, and yet another may hold body memory. Alters can also be created to hold repressed feelings, because emotions don't dissipate until they are processed. They must go somewhere. Therefore, you will find a full range of emotions in alters: angry alters, alters holding emotional pain, and parts that just feel sad. Alters tend to have jobs inside and sometimes specific roles, such as system protector. System protectors will valiantly serve to protect with whatever means necessary.

Finally, it's important to know how to identify preverbal alters. They can't tell you what is wrong and most of the time they are unable to move themselves forward on the internal stage. Preverbal alters function entirely in the right brain. They feel emotions powerfully and are highly intuitive. One way to identify them is by the pictures and feelings that come to mind. Babies do not have a sense of time, what they feel, they feel as though it will never end. If they are frightened, they experience the fear with every fiber of their being. If you sense you may be dealing with an infant alter simply ask Jesus to go get the baby and minister His healing. He is faithful.

Although SRA ministry training is beyond the scope of this text I can recommend you check out the Restoration Gateway Ministries advanced training resources at www.rgmconnect.com or materials from Diane Hawkins at Restoration in Christ Ministries www.rcm-usa.org for your continued study.

For more on basic DID healing, I have included a couple of examples for your reference, followed by a few simple steps you can put into practice.

EXAMPLES OF BASIC DID HEALING

Many years ago, I ministered to a young man whose mother brought him to see me. He was raised with strong Christian values but was struggling to cope in public high school. At seven years of age, his parents divorced. He was so torn emotionally between both parents that he literally split creating an alter to cope with the turmoil. Because splitting happened just before his personality was solid, he was capable of splitting again given the right circumstances. At fifteen he felt torn in a similar way between his Christian values at home and the culture of public high school. Again, he split to cope with the dichotomy. When I asked about these parts inside I found both a seven-year old alter and a fifteen-year-old alter, appropriately named "Compromise."

I asked Compromise to tell me what life in high school was like for him. He told me his job was to handle the hours at school while the main part of him was forward at home. He expressed how difficult it was to be a Christian around his friends at school. But he felt guilty for filthy language and other inappropriate behavior at home. We took some time to discuss creative ways to cope with his challenges both at home and at school. Then I asked Compromise if he was willing to integrate back into the place in the boy's heart where he had come. Compromise agreed. He went to Jesus inside. Jesus ministered His love and compassion, forgiveness, and understanding. Then Compromise stepped right back into the young man's heart. Pretty amazing!

The boy's mother is the next example. When she was a little girl she got into trouble for doing something she wasn't supposed to do. Her mother screamed and yelled at her and locked her in the bathroom until her father came home. Mom threatened that she was going to get a serious spanking as soon as Dad returned home from work. Meanwhile, she had hours to think about this pending event before Dad arrived home. To cope with the stress, she split.

I asked her, "Who inside was waiting for Daddy to come home?" A sweet little voice came forward and said, "It was me!" I asked her what her name was and she replied "Spanking." She went on to tell me that whenever she is bad she gets really scared because she is still waiting for a spanking.

I reassured the child that nobody was going to spank her. I explained that she had grown up and she was safe now. I apologized for mom's behavior and asked if the child would like to meet Jesus. Wholeheartedly she exclaimed, "Yes, I love Jesus!"

I suggested she look for Jesus inside. When she saw Him, she took His hand and He led her out of the scene in the bathroom, then He sat her on His lap. When He gave her a big hug she slipped right into Jesus, who was resident in the adult heart. Jesus is the Wonderful Counselor (Is. 9:6).

Integration in basic matters such as these can be very easy. However, integration ministry is far more complex when ritual abuse caused the splitting. For more information on SRA integration, contact Restoration Gateway Ministries through the website at www.rgmconnect.com.

BASIC INTEGRATION

I often pray Ephesians 1:17-18 before ministering, *"that the God of our LORD Jesus Christ, the Father of glory, may give to you the spirit of wisdom and revelation in the knowledge of Him, the eyes of your understanding being enlightened..."* It is amazing the revelation God will provide if you ask for it.

Reaching unprocessed trauma can be done in a variety of ways.

One method is to ask the client to focus on the feeling associated with an area of difficulty, such as the fear that keeps them awake. Next have them look inside to report what they see. Focusing on feelings and pictures will activate the right brain. Although the imagination is in the right brain, *repressed memory bypasses this function.*

Once the alters that need healing are identified, they may need to process a memory or problem solve an issue to resolve internal conflict. Ask the LORD to help you meet specific needs in the power of the Holy Spirit. When parts are ready for healing move on to these basic steps.

1. Facilitate connection between the ministry recipient and the LORD Jesus.
2. Invite the part or parts inside to release whatever they are holding to Jesus. Typically, they have movie reels or DVDs of trauma events as well as lots of big feelings. Have them picture feelings as objects that they can give Him.
3. Facilitate forgiveness, and if necessary, repentance (applicable to parts that are past the age of accountability).
4. Invite them to receive love and healing from Jesus.
5. While He is ministering gently bind and cast out demons on the alter(s).
6. Ask Jesus to restore the broken piece(s) of the heart.
7. Ask for an infilling of the Holy Spirit and offer praise for healing!

INTEGRATION RESISTANCE

Sometimes alters are afraid to integrate because they don't know what the word integrate means. With young alters it helps to describe the process like Play-Doh. The child part is one ball of Play-Doh and the adult is a bigger ball of Play-Doh. Integration is simply blending them together to make one ball. If they are different colors they maintain their special color. They don't go away, they are put back together.

In some instances, alters want to know who will do their job if they aren't there to do it. I recommend having them ask Jesus this question. Often, He will volunteer to serve in that role. For example, if a part is a protector, Jesus may reassure them that He will protect now.

Some trauma survivors have been abused by a man claiming to be Jesus. In this case, the part(s) may express fear about Jesus. It may help to explain that this is the real Jesus and the person who hurt them was just a man pretending to be Jesus. If this explanation doesn't work, other options include asking for an angel of the LORD to help or the Holy Spirit.

Integrations appear to take a little time to "set," sometimes a day or two. Very large integrations can take longer.

I like to picture my life as a water pitcher. I like water pitchers so much, I collect them in various sizes and colors, the prettier the better. When I came to Jesus, I was shattered and couldn't hold water. But like clay, He put me on the potter's wheel and gently, lovingly, reshaped my life with the skill of a master artisan. Now I can hold living water. I have integrity. The word integrity means more than honesty and moral uprightness. It is also the state of being whole and undivided. As we allow the LORD to mold our character, to reshape, and redefine us, we become a vessel of honor on the Master's table prepared for every good work (2 Timothy 2:21).

In 3 John 1:2, the word says, *"Beloved, I pray that you may prosper in all things and be in health, just as your soul prospers."* Healing of the soul is related to more than emotional healing, it is prosperity and physical health as well. Most importantly, restoration of the soul transforms lives and makes more room for Jesus.

CHAPTER 15

NEW WINESKIN MINISTRY

"And no one puts new wine into old wineskins; or else the new wine bursts the wineskins, the wine is spilled, and the wineskins are ruined. But new wine must be put into new wineskins."

Mark 2:22

The old wineskin for healing and deliverance can't hold what God has for us today. In greater measure than ever before God is releasing His anointing to accelerate the work of ministry. The bowls of heaven are tipping over with warm fresh oil. Like Aaron, let it pour over you. Receive it by faith.

"It shall come to pass in that day, that this burden will be taken away from your shoulder, and his yoke from your neck, and the yoke will be destroyed because of the anointing oil" (Isaiah 10:27).

What used to take years will be accomplished in hours. There is an acceleration from the throne room to redeem the time, heal the brokenhearted, and set the captives free. In the new wineskin, we host His presence which doesn't fit in the confines of our authority, our knowledge, or our identity from the past. It's not about us, it's about Him. Hearing His instructions and ministering out of His heart of compassion, we can expect miracles to happen.

"And His name will be called Wonderful, Counselor, Mighty God, Everlasting Father, Prince of Peace" (Isaiah 9:6).

KINGDOM EMOTIONS

Mark Virkler posted an article on the Elijah List, June 9, 2017, about Kingdom emotions. In it he says, "Heightened kingdom emotions become channels for the release of the power of the Spirit. Jesus, moved by compassion, healed (Matt.14:14). The power of the Spirit rode on the deep emotion of compassion." Further into the article he wrote, "It is time for the Church to embrace the place and role of intense Kingdom emotions birthed by the Spirit, rather than marginalizing emotions as being only soulish." Additionally, he said, "Kingdom emotions flow together with Kingdom actions."[11]

Lester Sumrall, in "The Gifts and Ministries of the Holy Spirit," wrote, "There must be love, pure love. Without it the spiritual gifts cannot function [properly]."

The compassion of Christ motivates and compels us to serve. As Christ pours His anointing into us, we, in turn, pour out on others, as vessels of honor on the Master's table (2 Timothy 2:21).

Human beings are such complex creatures. One size doesn't fit all when it comes to healing and deliverance. That's why we put our trust in Jesus and move as He moves, with compassion. We can't go wrong as Jesus with skin on.

EXAMPLE OF THE NEW WINESKIN IN MINISTRY

This story is a good illustration of the new wineskin in ministry. As you read it consider how you might have done things differently in the old wineskin and what you want to incorporate in the new. It was the end of a long day. I had ministered to several people

---

11   http://www.elijahlist.com/words/display_word.html?ID=18144

and I was tired. I remember thinking, "God if you don't show up nothing is going to happen here today and the person in front of me desperately needs a touch from you."

Beth (not her real name) sat uneasily on my big overstuffed couch. "You have no idea how hard it was to get here today," she stated. "I had to cross the Interstate Bridge and it was all I could do not to turn around and drive home."

"Oh" I replied surprised. "Are you uncomfortable with bridges or was it something else that bothered you?"

"I really have a problem with bridges. Actually, it's a fear of heights and bridges are high."

"I didn't know you had a fear of bridges," I replied. "When was the first time you recall feeling that way?"

Beth responded shaking her head, "I don't know, I've had it all my life. It's just gotten worse lately since I've been coming to see you."

"Hmmm." I pondered, resisting the urge to take her comment personally.

"There must be a good reason you felt so fearful. Do you remember anything related to bridges?"

Beth took a deep breath, "No, but I hate tall buildings and elevators too. For the life of me I could never get on an airplane."

"What happens when you feel so fearful?" I asked.

Beth said, "I just freeze. I can't move. My whole body gets stiff."

"Okay," I began. "That's an important clue. Did you know that human beings have three ways to respond to fear? They are fight, flight, or freeze. It sounds like you are not inclined to fight or run, instead you freeze, right?"

"Yes." She nodded.

I continued. "It may be helpful to know that our brain will respond to a trauma or threat in a similar way after the first event. So, if you consistently freeze that tells me you must have been very young when you first experienced this fear. Let's ask Jesus to reveal to us what happened."

I asked Beth to fix her eyes on Jesus and draw close to Him. "Let's ask Him to help us understand the problem."

She sat very still. Tears fell from her cheeks and she said, "I'm blank. I don't see anything. I don't hear anything, but I feel really scared and my body is stiff."

"Okay, stay with the feelings, let's give it a few more minutes, let me know what else you notice." I said.

Suddenly, she opened her eyes wide and said, "I just feel terrified, like I'm going to die!"

"Okay, stay with the feelings, I'm right here with you."

She closed her eyes again while I prayed, "Jesus, please show her what she needs to know."

Moments later she began sobbing. "I feel like I'm falling!" she cried. "I can't even breathe!"

I said calmly, "You are remembering."

Beth described experiencing herself as an infant being tossed from one man to the next in a large circle of men like a football. When they threw her tiny body into the air every muscle became rigid with terror.

In those moments with me, Beth was processing both the memory and the emotions.

Next, I asked her if Jesus could hold the tiny baby girl inside that had been tossed in the air. She nodded her head "yes". On the screen in her mind she could see Jesus holding the baby and comforting her. I asked Jesus to lift the trauma memory and heal the baby. He kept saying to her, "You're safe now little one."

Then, in a gentle, soft voice, I commanded every spirit that entered this child when she was tossed to evacuate in Jesus name. "Every spirit of fear, go!" I said.

I didn't have to name every devil; there was no fighting with the spirits and I didn't have to ask this woman to repent for being fearful when she was preverbal.

When the healing came to the emotional wound the spirits had no place to cleave and they left quietly and peacefully. The LORD, reunited this fractured part of Beth's heart back into Beth. He supernaturally matured the infant part and the healing was made manifest.

It was obvious that her fear of bridges had nothing to do with bridges. It really had to do with a fear of falling as the result of this traumatic preverbal event. After this ministry session Beth reported being able to cross bridges without freezing or feeling fearful. She literally crossed over into victory!

In the old wineskin, we might approach this problem as a

stronghold of fear. Indeed, there was a stronghold of fear. But the real issue wasn't the demons, although they were there. The issue was the trauma memory undergirding the stronghold and a preverbal alter identity. Had I not ministered to the infant alter the trauma memory would have remained and the fear along with it.

Is it possible that Beth might feel fearful again around heights? Yes, there could have been multiple incidents during her lifetime that induced that fear. For most people, an issue this significant isn't usually resolved by healing a single incident. Many times, there are layers to the onion that need to be gently peeled back, one at a time. As the soul heals the freedom comes.

CONCLUSION

When I walked through my healing journey the LORD in His mercy took me along the long hard route. He designed me with the spirit of a pioneer and He knew that if I walked through problems myself I would become equipped to help someone else. On my quest to freedom and wholeness I couldn't leave a stone unturned. Nearly thirty years later, I can look back and see the value in those long circuitous roads, the deep valleys, and the steep assent through the mountains of perseverance that tested my faith and my resolve. There was value in it all. I hope you too will allow Jesus to take everything you've experienced, and everything you've learned, to that mountain top of triumph.

The new wineskin for healing and deliverance is not a long list of protocols or a lengthy task list. It can only be found in Him, by His Spirit. As conduits of His power we move and have our being in Him. Our identity firmly grounded as a son or daughter of the Most High God, we are humble and obedient with ears to hear the Holy Spirit. We create emotional safety and develop good listening skills. Legalism, judgment, and spiritual abuse are things of the past. We operate in strong emotional intelligence, enabling us to move with compassion like Jesus.

Formerly, I called myself a deliverance minister. But today, I am a minister of Jesus Christ. There is so much more to Him than a single facet of ministry. Jesus is all encompassing and He supplies all our needs according to His riches and glory (Philippians 4:19). It is my hope after reading this text, you will allow the compassion of Jesus to overwhelm you, as you reach out to the brokenhearted and bring freedom to the captives.

"So, chosen by God for this new life of love, dress in the wardrobe God picked out for you: compassion, kindness, humility, quiet strength, discipline. Be even-tempered, content with second place, quick to forgive an offense. Forgive as quickly and completely as the Master forgave you. And regardless of what else you put on, wear love. It's your basic, all-purpose garment. Never be without it."

Colossians 3:12-14 - The Message Bible

WORKS CITED

American Psychiatric Association. The Diagnostic and Statistical Manual of Mental Disorders-IV, 4th edition. Washington, DC. American Psychiatric Association. 1994.

Covey, Stephen R. The 7 Habits of Highly Effective People. New York, NY: Fireside, 1989.

Davis, Timothy. Cleansing Streams Seminar Workbook. Cleansing Streams Ministries.

Dictionary.com. http://www.dictionary.com/browse/pharisaical. June 29, 2017. Web.

Eberle Ph.D., Harold. Systematic Theology for the New Apostolic Reformation; An Exposition in Father-Son Theology. Yakima, WA. Worldcast Publishing. 2015.

Elwell, Walter, A. Baker's Evangelical Dictionary of Biblical Theology. http://www.biblestudytools.com/dictionary/mercy/ August 12, 2017. Web.

Greater Good Magazine. Published by UC Berkley. http://greatergood.berkeley.edu/topic/compassion/definition. Dec. 15, 2016. Web.

Haddock, Deborah Bray, M.Ed., M.A., L.P. The Dissociative Identity Disorder Sourcebook. New York, NY. McGraw-Hill Companies, Inc. 2001.

Haugk Ph.D., Kenneth C. Don't Sing Songs to A Heavy Heart. St.

Louis, MO. Stephen Ministries, 2004.

Hayford, Litt.D., Jack W. (Executive Editor). New Spirit Filled Life Bible – NKJV. Nashville, TN. Thomas Nelson, Inc. 2002.

Hegstrom Ph.D., Paul Broken Children, Grown-up Pain; Understanding the Effects of Your Wounded Past. Kansas City, MO. Beacon Hill Press. 2001, 2006.

Henderson, Robert. Operating in the Courts of Heaven. Robert Henderson Ministries. 2014.

Jones, Bob. Elijah List http://www.elijahlist.com/words/display_ word.html?ID=13128. June 9, 2017. Web.

Joyner, Rick. There Were Two Trees in the Garden. Fort Mill, SC. MorningStar Publications, Inc. 1985.

Kubler-Ross MD., Elizabeth. On Death and Dying. 1969.

Leaf Ph.D., Carolyn Who Switched Off My Brain? South Lake, TX. Inprov, Ltd., 2009.

Luscombe, Belinda. "Let's Talk About Grief." Time Magazine, April 24, 2017.

Maston, Luke. The Basics of Philosophy. http://www. philosophybasics.com/branch_stoicism.html. Dec. 1, 2016. Web. Meyer, Joyce. The Everyday Life Bible, Amplified Version. New York, NY. Faith Words. 2006.

Meyer, Joyce. Living Beyond Your Feelings; Controlling Emotions So They Don't Control You. New York, NY. Faith Words. 2011.

Merriam-Webster Dictionary. https://www.merriam-webster.com/

dictionary/compassion. March 1, 2017. Web.

National Institute for Mental Health. Post-Traumatic Stress Disorder. https://www.nimh.nih.gov/health/topics/post-traumatic-stress-disorder-ptsd/index.shtml. August 15, 2017. Web.

New American Standard Bible. La Habra, CA. The Lockman Foundation, 1977

Peterson, Eugene H. The Message Bible; The Bible in Contemporary Language. NavPress Publishing Group. 1993, 1994, 1995, 1996, 2000, 2001, 2002,

Shiva.com. The Resource for Jewish Mourning. http://www.shiva.com/learning-center/understanding/periods-of-mourning/. March 1, 2017. Web.

Strong, James. Strong's Exhaustive Concordance of the Bible. Peabody, MA. Hendrickson Publishers, Inc. 2009.

Sumrall, Lester. The Gifts and Ministries of the Holy Spirit. New Kensington, PA. Whitaker House. 1982.

Van Der Kolk, MD., Bessel. The Body Keeps the Score; Brain, Mind, And Body in the Healing of Trauma. New York, NY. Penguin Books. 2014.

Virkler, Mark & Patti. 4 Keys to Hearing God's Voice. Shippensburg, PA. Destiny Image Publishers, Inc. 2010.

Virkler, Mark. When God Roars the Enemy is Destroyed. Elijah List. http://www.elijahlist.com/words/display_word.html?ID=18144. June 9, 2017. Web.

Wikipedia. https://en.wikipedia.org/wiki/Stoicism. December 15,

2016. Web.

Wright, Henry W. A More Excellent Way; Be in Health. Thomaston, GA. Pleasant Valley Church, Inc. 2007.

MINISTRY RESOURCES

Communion with God Ministries: www.cwgministries.org - 4 Keys to Hearing God's Voice and the ministry of Dr. Mark Virkler

Elijah House Ministries: www.elijahhouse.org – Bitter Root Judgments from John and Paula Sandford

Fruitful Vine: wwwfruitfulvine.org – Deliverance materials from Yvonne Kitchen

Global Awakenings: www.goglobal@globalawakening.com – PTSD from Dr. Mike Hutchings

Kanaan Ministries: www.kanaanministries.org – Deliverance materials from Amanda Buys

Mastering Life Ministries: http://purepassion.us - Sexual healing from David Kyle Foster

Restoration in Christ Ministries: www.rcm-usa.org – DID from Dianne Hawkins

Restoration Gateway Ministries: www.rgmconnect.com – Healing & Deliverance from Kay Tolman

ABOUT THE AUTHOR

Kay Tolman is the Founder and President of Restoration Gateway Ministries, in Portland, Oregon. She has been commissioned by Glory of Zion International and Global Spheres Inc. She also serves the Reformation Prayer Network as a General for the State of Oregon.

With a Master of Christian Counseling degree from Christian Leadership University, Kay specializes in the restoration of severe trauma survivors, and the training and equipping of Christian ministers both nationally and internationally.

She is the author of *Satanic Ritual Abuse Exposed; Recovery of a Christian Survivor.*

Kay and her husband Ryan have been married for nearly 30 years. They have four adult children and four grandchildren in the Pacific Northwest.

CONNECT WITH KAY

www.rgmconnect.com
info@rgmconnect.com